SANDRA FINLEY DORAN

NOBODY'S BOY

This edition of *Nobody's Boy* has been especially printed for the *It Is Written* telecast hosted by Mark A. Finley. *It Is Written* is a ministry of the Seventh-day Adventist Church.

TO HOLLY

*who laughed, sighed, and wept
at all the right places.*

*The following is a true story. Of necessity, some of the
names of people, places, and companies have been
changed.*

Copyright © 1982 by the
Review and Herald Publishing Association

Copyright © 1994 by
Sandra Doran

Editor: Bobbie Jane Van Dolson
Book Design: Robert Wright

Cover Illustration by Bobbi Tull

Printed in U.S.A.

Library of Congress Cataloging in Publication Data

Doran, Sandra Finley, 1954-
    Nobody's boy.

    1. Finley, James, 1923-   2. Converts, Seventh-day
Adventist—United States—Biography.
I. Title
BX6193.F56D67   248.2'46   81-23368
ISBN 0-8280-0111-1   AACR2

CONTENTS

Miles to Go 9
Hell's Kitchen 14
Harlem 20
Brooklyn and Back 25
Coney Island Behind 31
New London and West 36
Mare Island and Holding 43
San Diego and Onward 48
New England to Stay 54
New Life at 33 60
No Key to Easy Street 66
One-time Altar Boy 72
A Family United 79
Build Your Own Dynasty 85
Sum of the Parts 89
Happiness 94

Preface

As I have looked back over my life and realized how the Lord has personally loved and cared for me I have felt a need to share my story with others, to encourage them in their lives. Several groups of people in particular may find something in these pages to make their step a bit lighter and their perception of God's love for them a bit clearer.

First, I have related the events of my life to my daughter, to portray in these pages a message of hope for the youth in the slums—to let them know that there is a way out, a God who loves and cares for them more than they can ever know.

Next, I wanted to remind those whose marriage partner is of another faith that God loves both of them and that when two people return that love to Him and then to each other, He will not forsake them.

Last, I wanted to let the businessman know that faith in God will guide him in all his decisions.

And I must remind all who are searching for God's light and truth that motive is important. Believing in God is not a good-luck charm—but a charm when bad luck comes your way!

James Finley
October, 1981

Miles to Go

Dark, dripping trees, blurred masses of houses, fields, hills—framed by a wet window. Jim's thoughts were like the passing scenery—hazy and changing, misting over with fears and uncertainties.

Maybe they would want him. Maybe it would work this time. Maybe he could settle down and stop the constant moving, the endless changing of hands: Atlanta to New Jersey, New Jersey to Somerville, Somerville to Chattanooga, and now Chattanooga to New York City.

He would miss Milton. Milton had been about his age. But he had no regrets about leaving his aunt and uncle, with their stern faces and strict rules. He remembered the few times his mother had visited and how she had to hide in the bedroom so that his uncle would not see her reading the paper on Sunday. He remembered the small country town and waiting in the car during the tent meetings, cabin churches, and hospital visits that were all part of his uncle's life as a Protestant minister. And he remembered the beatings and harsh words, the resultant feelings of anger, despair, and emptiness.

Jim hadn't meant to make his uncle angry so many times—things just seemed to happen that way. Like that time they had the party for him. Uncle Harold had told him who to ask, but he didn't think anybody would mind if Joey came. Sure, Joey dressed kinda funny, and he didn't live in a very nice house, but after all, Joey was his friend. Jim had been upstairs getting ready when Joey got there. He hadn't seen the look on his uncle's face when he let him in, but Joey didn't stay too long. Uncle Harold took care of that.

Jim straightened up in his seat and turned his gaze away from the dripping scenery to the inside of the train. A blur of colors and

NOBODY'S BOY

sounds vibrated all around him, yet he was not part of it. White-haired gentlemen, crying babies, angry mothers, laughing lovers, and sleeping children blended into one united whole, living and breathing in a world he could not enter. He felt empty, hollow, an outcast—a boy of 10, traveling not as a beloved grandchild, pleasant companion, or even annoying son, but alone. He was without a role, without a purpose—a burden being shifted from back to back, carried only until his weight became too heavy.

This time they were passing him to his mother. He didn't know the identity of his father, and never would. He bore the last name of a man his young mother had married after his birth: David Finley. Mr. Finley was twenty-five years older than his mother, and a Yankee at that! But he would learn to call him Dad. He would have to.

Abruptly the conductor's voice broke into Jim's thoughts. "Last stop, Washington, D.C.! Everybody off!"

The passengers reached for carrying cases, pocketbooks, and briefcases as they buzzed excitedly in anticipation of their visits or homecomings. Jim must change trains. The thought frightened him, but he gripped his bag and stood up with the eager crowd. He felt numb after hours of sitting. His head throbbed dizzily, and he hoped he could manage. They had said a Traveler's Aid would be here to help him. But how could he be sure of anything?

He climbed down the stairs, and the surging crowd pulled him forward. There was an empty place on one bench, and he made for it. Sitting beside a smiling mother and her son, he thought passers-by might consider him part of a family. But the next instant woman and boy were running happily toward a tanned blond man. The perfect family reunion. How would his own be?

When he turned back, a trim brunette woman in a tailored blue uniform was watching him carefully. He was dressed very neatly in laced brown shoes, knee socks, brown shorts, white shirt, and even a tie. His blond hair was cut short above the ears and combed smoothly to the side. His eyes looked at the woman questioningly through dark-rimmed round glasses—glasses that

MILES TO GO

somehow shielded his sensitive face, shutting him out somewhat from the noise of the people all about him. The woman smiled, not a pitying smile as he had expected, but one that almost seemed to signify respect.

"James Finley?" Her voice had no edge of condescension.

"Yes, ma'am."

"I'm Joan Adams, your Traveler's Aid. Your next train will be leaving in a little more than an hour."

Jim wondered how she'd been able to spot him in the crowd. Maybe they'd sent his picture or something. She seemed friendly. It was good to have someone to talk to.

"Would you like to get up and walk around a bit? You must have been sitting for an awfully long time, riding all the way from Tennessee." She looked down at Jim.

Had they told her he was from Tennessee, or was his accent giving him away? He hadn't realized he had an accent until he heard her voice.

"That would be nice, ma'am," he said, trying to sound polite. It would have been nicer just to rest somewhere. Even though he'd been sitting for twelve hours, he didn't feel the need to stretch. He felt tired and groggy. But Joan Adams walked briskly, and he hurried to catch up.

Although the rain had stopped, the sky still held no promise of blue. Small gusts of wind blew bits of paper about and brushed his bangs against his forehead. His numbness was being gradually replaced by an awakening of the senses, and he remembered it had been a while since he'd eaten. Uncle Harold had given him a little money for food.

"Miss Adams, do you think I could stop somewhere and get something to eat?" Jim tried not to sound too anxious.

She smiled at him, revealing a set of straight white teeth.

"Of course. What sounds good to you?"

"Do they sell hot dogs around here?"

"Sure, that's a universal favorite. Come on, I'll take you to Joe's. They have the best hot dogs in town!" She spoke lightly in a carefree style he was not used to. He wondered whether she ever worried about things like budgets, bills, being sick, or losing her soul.

NOBODY'S BOY

The meal passed quickly, and with it the hour of respite from the dulling journey. From the train he watched as Miss Adams' waving hand faded out of sight, and once again he settled back in his seat as an anonymous stranger in an indifferent crowd.

He thought about her for a while—was she nice only to strangers? Was there a reason for her good mood or was she always like that? He wondered what she did when she was upset—whether she ever got upset. He recalled his uncle's anger the time when the key got buried too deep. Jim hadn't done it on purpose. They always kept the key in the flowerpot. He knew he was supposed to bury it there after he used it, and he had just wanted to make sure it wouldn't fall out. He had figured if he buried it as deep as he could, nothing would happen to it. He hadn't realized they'd want to get in the house in a hurry and wouldn't be able to find it. Would Miss Adams have been as angry as Uncle Harold? Would she have been determined to set him straight for his tomfoolery? He didn't think so. No, she probably would have just smiled or even laughed.

But everybody got angry once in a while. Surely Miss Adams wasn't perfect. She'd probably have given it to him the time he came home with his new riding pants wrecked. After all, they were a present and brand-new—never been worn. He should have been more careful, even though Charlie was the one who had picked the fight with him. He could have gotten out of it somehow or at least stood up for himself. If he had given it to Charlie right from the beginning, he wouldn't have been knocked down and Charlie couldn't have wiped up the whole school yard with him. He tried to give him one in the nose, but he was scared, and, besides, Charlie was a lot bigger. Jim straightened up and pounded his fists into the seat in front of him. Well, he should have known better than to wear his new riding pants around Charlie's house anyway. Yes, Miss Adams would've been angry about that. Nobody's perfect.

Even principals aren't perfect. Jim hadn't known why the teacher made him stand out in the hall. But the principal said he must know. He said every boy standing out in the hall knew very well that it was because he was bad. But Jim really didn't know what he had done wrong. The principal said if he didn't want to

12

MILES TO GO

tell why he was standing out in the hall, then they'd just have to go right into the classroom and ask his teacher. He was scared when the principal opened the door. But then they yelled "Surprise!" At first he didn't understand. But then someone started singing "For He's a Jolly Good Fellow," and they all yelled out, "We're gonna miss you, Jimmy!" A going-away party—for him! It had almost made him want to stay.

He laid his head back on the seat and closed his eyes. The train rolled on, its wheels beating out the cadence of his troubled sleep.

When he awoke, someone was shaking him.

"Last stop, sonny. Jersey City. Ain't you gettin' off?"

He looked around frightened. The other seats were empty. Was this where they said to get off? The conductor motioned him to the door, and with shaking legs he stepped from the train.

People bustled in every direction. Suddenly he knew no one would be there to meet him. With the weight of the trip heavy upon him and the fear of being lost in a strange, crowded city, the reserve of ten hard years fell away, and he began to cry.

He felt a gentle hand on his shoulder and allowed himself to be led into the depot. He told them his name and waited while phone calls were made. He listened while they explained, and once again he was on his journey. Wrong stop . . . should have been New York City . . . a half-hour bus ride.

He was scared now. He didn't want to live in the city. It didn't matter if Uncle Harold beat him once in a while. He hoped the bus ride would last a long time. He hoped it would last forever. He couldn't face that crowd again. His mother didn't care. She wouldn't be there.

"Thirty-fourth Street—here's where you get off, buddy."

He gripped the railing with a sweaty hand as he went down the steps. People, more people than he had ever seen before, milled about in every direction. He recognized no one. He looked about in despair until he saw her striding heavily toward him. Beulah Finley had come to meet her son, who involuntarily turned his back and ran away from her into the surging crowd.

13

Hell's Kitchen

James! James! Come back!"

Jim heard her voice as if it were coming from the end of a long tunnel. He found himself turning obediently and walking toward her. There was nowhere else to go.

He looked at her, not as a boy seeing his mother, but as a stranger observing a newcomer. Beulah was a heavy woman, with dark-brown hair curling away from her wide face. Her navy-blue dress had faded in spots and begun to ravel at the ends of the sleeves.

"Don't you love your own mamma anymore?" Tears rolled down the fat cheeks as she held out her arms pleadingly.

He felt himself falling and then sheltered as she hugged him to her massive body. He wanted to tell her that the trip had done it. He hadn't meant to run, but he'd been riding so long, and he felt so dizzy, and there were so many people, and it was so hot here. But the words wouldn't come.

"James! My very own James! Aren't you glad to see me?"

He looked down at the sidewalk. "Yes, ma'am."

The taxi ride to Forty-sixth Street passed in a blur. Jim stepped out and viewed his new neighborhood—Hell's Kitchen, New York City. It was all the name implied.

Hungry, grimy children and dogs romped and fought on the sidewalk in front of the crowded line of apartments. No hint of grass or trees added a softening touch of green to the maze of cement and stone. The Southern back yards to which he was accustomed were replaced here by alleys running crookedly behind the tightly packed buildings.

His mother took his hand firmly, and they walked into the gloom of the ten-family brownstone apartment building. In their quarters she motioned to a small space off the kitchen.

HELL'S KITCHEN

"Here's your room, James. Bet you're awfully tired right now, you poor thing . . ."

When she left, he closed the door gratefully and lay down on the bed. He heard voices outside the room, but didn't care who they belonged to.

He awoke to the sound of forks clinking against plates. Sitting up groggily, he surveyed the chipped plaster, battered dresser, and small window for a moment before recognition came. Then he eased himself to the floor and walked quietly to the kitchen.

"We-ell, good to see ya, James!" David Finley stood up and greeted his stepson while Beulah pulled out a chair. "Plenty of chicken left. Beulah, fix a plate for James." The boy felt like an honored guest as he watched his plate being heaped with mashed potatoes, golden fried chicken, string beans, and bread.

"My, you're quiet, James. What's the matter? Why, you know us all here—your own mamma and papa, your stepbrother, Dave, and his wife, Lilly, and Ed. Oh, that's right—Ed. He's our boarder. Is he what's scarin' you?" His mother looked coyly in the direction of a short, dark-haired man, and they all laughed.

Jim looked at his plate. He wanted to talk to her, tell her she was a good cook, ask his brother what he'd been doing lately, ask his stepfather about the tugs. But they were all looking at him, and at Uncle Harold's you weren't supposed to do a lot of talking when you were eating anyway.

"The chicken's mighty good, ma'am," he managed.

The next morning the sun rose early, determined and bright, before the night breezes had time to cool off the city. When Jim could bear the stuffiness of the small room no longer, he quickly washed and dressed and slipped out the front door.

He wanted to think—to escape the uncomfortable feeling he got while cooped up in the apartment with his relatives. He didn't know whether they really wanted him here. The smiles, the words, the gestures, all seemed like thin, sugary coatings ready to crack at any moment, revealing ugliness within.

He shuffled on, head down, out of touch with the yelling

15

NOBODY'S BOY

children and peeling billboards around him. A rough hand pushed him into a brick wall. He looked up, eyes blinking rapidly, hands reaching out for something to grab onto.

"You the Southernah we heard was movin' in around here?"

The five boys pushed in closer, leering at him.

He tried to talk, but no answer came.

"Lissen, Mac. We wanna hear ya talk. We ain't heard no rebels for a l-o-o-o-ng time."

He directed his voice to the ground. "Why don't ya'll leave me alone?"

The tall skinny boy moved in a step closer. "Did you hear that? I think we got us a sissy here, *y'all!*" His rocklike fist slammed into Jim's stomach, and the others laughed with delight at this new diversion from monotony. A hand stung the boy's face, a heel caught his knee, a knuckle jammed into his jaw. When they left, he was feebly aware of the warm blood trickling down his face. Crying, he headed for the only place he could call home.

His stepfather saw him first.

"What happened, James? W-e-ll, looks to me like you been beat up. Don't you come home like that. You git yourself back out there, and you beat the tar out o' whoever done that to you. And don't you come home until you do. You hear me, James?"

"Yes, sir." Jim limped back down the street, anger welling up within him. Nobody was on his side. Nobody liked him, nobody cared. Well, he didn't care either—didn't care about what Uncle Harold had told him about fighting being sinful, didn't care that nobody was there to wipe up his blood and tears, didn't care that he was different, laughed at, ignored.

Just then his eye caught a glimpse of the skinny kid leaning against a brick wall—alone. With all his might, he charged, slamming his body full force into the gaunt back, grabbing, pushing, smashing, until the wall was stained with the skinny boy's blood. Proudly he turned homeward, not knowing that One had shed His blood to save him from such a meaningless pride.

A few days later Jim's stepbrother, Dave, suggested he go to

HELL'S KITCHEN

the gym on top of the Hartley House and shoot some baskets. Glad for a chance to get out of the apartment, Jim walked the few blocks—this time not with his head down, but cocked warily to the side. He was looking out for himself. At the Hartley House he met a few friends from his street. Fontaine threw Jim the ball, and he joined in the game. They played for about an hour. Then McIntyre threw the ball to Fontaine. "Let's go."

Jim wanted to take one more shot. "Fontaine, right here!"

He held up his hands for the ball, caught it, and dribbled it around for a few moments. Just as he was ready to shoot, he noticed that every boy in the place was running for the fire escape. He scanned the room for his friends and saw them in front of the crowd, almost to the door. "McIntyre, Fontaine, what's going on?" He began running with the others, knowing he had to get out, but not knowing why.

"Last one out always gets beat up!" A fat kid in a yellow T-shirt was trying to get past him. Jim began squeezing, pushing, running, falling, down the iron steps. His feet hit the cement seconds before the yellow T-shirt lunged past him. The crowd pummeled the unfortunate last one, until the blood dripped and ran off the white rolls of fat.

Despite his recent bravado, something within Jim recoiled at the sight. Dave could not understand why he never went to shoot baskets at the Hartley Gym again.

Life in Hell's Kitchen moved on, molding and shaping Jim into its style, until its ways became routine, and Southern life a rapidly fading memory. No longer did the boy think about settling down, but accepted the constant moving that accompanied his father's jobs and his mother's whims. He came to know the pattern: bad times, no work on the tugboats—moving to an apartment building where his father could do janitorial work in exchange for a place to live; things looking up, a need for tugboat captains—moving out of the janitor's apartment. But he knew enough not to expect to stay there long: trouble with the neighbors, his mother exaggerating problems to his angry father—time to move. And so the cycle went on: Forty-sixth Street to Sixteenth Street to Twenty-first Street to Forty-sixth

NOBODY'S BOY

Street (again) to Forty-fourth Street . . .

Jim overcame his initial shock at city life and learned to laugh at his father's nightly janitorial duty of taking out the garbage and throwing out the bums sprawled in the halls of the apartment building. He learned to hide his embarrassment when he stood in line for the free cans of beans and stew, wore the khaki pants that announced to the world he was on home relief, and made his stops at the Salvation Army for day-old bread and used clothes.

However, a few bright spots did shine through the grayness of routine days. Jim found that not all of life caused shame, hurt, and emptiness; that there *were* people—good people, kind people—who would take the time to stoop down and smile moments of happiness into a boy's life. He was reminded of this one day as he performed his small-paying job of escorting a blind woman who made slipcovers for the furniture in the dressing rooms of a theater. As he was about to leave, a short man tapped him on the shoulder.

"Would you please stay here a moment, young man? Someone wishes to see you."

Jim waited, leaning against the wall, eyebrows knit together in puzzled curiosity. He heard footsteps approaching and looked up. A man with a big nose shook his hand.

"I've seen you here many times helping a poor blind lady, doing a good job. I'm proud of you, son. It's boys like you who give me hope for tomorrow." Jimmy Durante handed him a silver dollar, smiled his warmest, and was on his way. Jim gazed after the star until he disappeared from view. His hand tightened around the silver dollar, holding the solid metal close while the fingers of his mind sought to tighten around the fleeting moment of kindness, grasp its warmth close to his being, and hold it there for a long time.

Others too sought to brighten Jim's existence. He looked forward to Friday nights, when someone from the Salvation Army would pick him up, buy him a candy bar, and bring him to a preaching session. He relished every last morsel of the candy and tolerated the preaching as part of the bargain. After

HELL'S KITCHEN

attending several Friday-night sessions, he took up the French horn. His mother tried to discourage him, claiming that he had only one lung and was too sick to play the instrument, but he was not bothered by her threats, and went on to play in the Salvation Army band.

One Friday night, just as he finished playing a number with the band in Times Square, the leader asked for people to give testimonies. Jim looked around at the scattered group attracted by the music, now eagerly listening for some words of encouragement. Not knowing why, he strode to the center of the group, and stepped up onto the soapbox.

"It's not easy for a guy like me to get up here, 'cause I ain't no better than the rest of you." All traces of Southern speech had vanished, erased by his three years in Hell's Kitchen.

"The only reason I got up here is 'cause I been goin' to the preachin' sessions at the Salvation Army for a few months now and I ain't always been listenin', but some of it's been sinkin' in. And I just gotta say that I think there's somethin' to this religion bit and someday I'm gonna find out what it is . . . and I hope that all of you do too."

He jumped down from the soapbox, heart pounding, brain spinning—trying to sort out what he had said, wondering even at his own words. He only knew it had been a case of necessity. He had to share it, tell somebody, before the feeling left him and became only a jagged memory too complicated to put together with the pieces of his life. He ran the five blocks home and was out of breath by the time he reached his front door. His hand flew for the doorknob, but it refused to turn. A white piece of paper, taped to the middle of the door, bore a scribbled message:

"We moved. New address: 110th Street, Harlem."

Harlem

Harlem overshadowed Hell's Kitchen. It looked down at her depravity and smirked, proud of its own greater affliction. While Hell's Kitchen boasted fights, dirt, and poverty, Harlem flaunted gang wars, filth, and destitution. Harlem was Hell's Kitchen intensified.

In the struggle to adjust to yet another new environment, Jim forgot about Times Square, the soapbox, and his trembling testimony. Of necessity, he directed all his energies to coping, relating, and surviving.

Homelife, too, was becoming harder to endure. The small bits of attention Jim had received from his mother and stepfather had ceased with the arrival of a baby brother. He felt as if he'd been born twelve years too early as he witnessed all the doting, attention, and praise showered upon little John. Jim could no longer escape from the oppressiveness he felt in the house, for it was impossible for him to be alone anywhere. Wherever he went, John wanted to follow. He didn't hate John, but rather resented the child's intrusion into the new life style to which he was struggling to adapt. Just when he had learned to be tough, to spend most of his time away from home with his friends, John arrived to tie him down. Jim became more tense, more anxious around the house. Every day he found himself trying to sneak away before hearing the demanding voice:

"James, you get back here this minute! Don't you love your little brother? Why do you want to make the poor little thing cry? Here's his coat. I can't understand why you don't act nicer to your own brother."

Beulah loved John, but she didn't always want him around. Especially not when Frank was coming. Frank had a Packard and worked for an insurance company. Sometimes, if Jim was

HARLEM

still around when Frank got there, the man would give him money to go to the show. But Jim hated him, hated the way he turned up when David Finley wasn't around, hated the way he followed the family from neighborhood to neighborhood and the way he showed off about money. The Finleys barely knew whether *they'd* have enough money to be able to eat for another week as David had again been laid off his job as a tugboat captain and had had to go into janitorial work. He received no income as a janitor—only free rent. They took in a young boarder, Donald Miller, whose mother worked in the sideshows at Coney Island. Every Sunday she telegraphed them fifteen dollars. The family waited anxiously each Sunday, knowing that if the money didn't come, they wouldn't eat; but she never missed. Although Donald was nearly 12, something about him made Jim feel a need to take care of him. One day, as Jim stood watching Donald bouncing a ball, a big boy from another neighborhood grabbed the ball and threw it over the roof.

Jim glared at the bold face. "Why did you do that?"

The boy met the challenge. "You wait here a minute and I'll show you why." He ran up and down the street, announcing to all his friends: "Come watch me beat a kid up good!"

Breathless now, he ran back to Jim. The crowd of boys formed a circle around the two fighters, jeering them on.

"Come on, Joe, let 'im have it!"

"Give it to 'im!"

Jim didn't like the taunting words. He didn't feel like fighting. Why had he gotten himself into this? His father would be mad. Well, it was too late to turn back now. He fought back the fear that pricked at his neck, and put up his fists.

Joe smelled success. This kid couldn't fight. Why, all he had to do was charge and he'd have him down.

"Come on, Joe, you can do it!"

The bigger boy charged toward Jim with all his might, head down as a bull seeing red. His head struck the clenched fists full force. He slumped to the ground, out cold.

The crowd broke up, disappointed.

"I thought Joe could do it."

"Yeah. Ya can never trust a guy smaller than you."

21

NOBODY'S BOY

Jim stood rooted to the spot in disbelief. A sick feeling was growing in the pit of his stomach, spreading, engulfing his whole body with trembling. He wanted to be proud. He thought of the first kid he had beat up in Hell's Kitchen, of the feeling of pride, of knowing he could take care of himself. But he couldn't awaken that feeling now. The boy on the ground didn't move. Donald Miller, crying, turned to Jim.

"Thanks a lot, Whitey." He used the nickname Jim's friends had given him because of his light hair. "You risked your neck for me. An' it's not over yet, 'cause here come your folks."

Donald turned and headed for the house. Jim stood alone, wishing with all his might that they didn't have to find out, that he could run far away and never come back. Already it was too late; already he heard his mother's voice.

"What on earth did you do, James? What was all that commotion out here? Do you mean to tell me you've gone and beat up a boy? Well, you're gonna get it good. I don't want any child of mine turning out to be a gangster. You get in the house this minute!"

But before he could obey the command, David Finley's voice intervened.

"The boy ain't done nothin' wrong. It's about time he became a man."

Jim looked at his stepfather, unbelieving. He could never remember him taking his side before. And talking to his mother like that! The boy on the ground was stirring. David Finley grabbed him by the shoulders and stood him up.

Listen to me, boy. You get yourself home and don't you ever come botherin' us around this street again." He gave him a sharp shove, and the defeated boy weaved his way down the alley.

Jim remembered the incident with a small glow. He had something to be proud of: his stepfather stood up for him. His stepfather at least cared enough to save him from his mother's wrath this once.

That Christmas David Finley got Jim a bike. The boy couldn't remember ever feeling so happy in all his life. That bike became his wings, his freedom. He rode the whole length of

22

HARLEM

Brooklyn. He pedaled over into New Jersey. His friend Pete Darogoth stole a bike parked in front of a candy store, and they took long trips together. They stole milk from trucks, slept in the woods, stayed away for days. Pete's philosophy of life was simple. As he explained to Whitey one day: "If people's rich, they can afford to help the poor. It don't matter if you take stuff from them. They got enough money to buy more."

Jim laughed. "I guess that's right." But inside he knew it wasn't.

He stopped by to get Pete one day and heard loud yells coming from his apartment. A pudgy face, framed with wire curlers, appeared at the window.

"Whitey, you're the one that made my boy bad!" Pete's mother slammed the window shut. Her words cut deep. He didn't mean to make other people bad. He didn't even mean to make himself bad. It just seemed to happen that way. He trudged home, head down, kicking a dented can. He pulled his bike up the four flights of stairs. When he heard the frenzied voices, he didn't want to go in. He didn't feel like listening to his mother. He turned to leave, but she opened the door.

"James, get in here right now. Your father and I have been looking for you. We've gotta get you to the hospital right away!"

The hospital?

"We just called the ambulance. Now pack your stuff, quick!"

He sat down on a wobbly kitchen chair.

"Stop being so stubborn and do what I say, James! John's got scarlet fever. How do we know you don't have it too? Even Donald's gotta go, to be on the safe side."

Beulah Finley was hysterical. Beads of sweat glistened on her upper lip. Her fat fingers clutched at a handkerchief. His stepfather said nothing.

Three days later, after being confined to Willard Parker Hospital and having been exposed to extremely contagious diseases, Jim and Donald were sent home on the subway. Suddenly Jim began to laugh. He laughed till the tears rolled down his cheeks. Donald eyed him curiously.

"What's so funny?"

"Here John gets sick, and they're so afraid we're gonna

23

NOBODY'S BOY

catch somethin' they keep John home and ship us off to a contagious hospital . . ." Jim choked again on giggles, and Donald looked at him incredulously. "And then they turn us loose on a subway to infect the rest of New York!"

The joke was on them. He saved it in the back of his mind, and whenever he needed a good laugh he recalled it, enjoying the absurdity of the situation over and over again.

A few days later his stepfather had good news. Jim heard it in his whistle as he climbed the stairs. He saw it shining out of his blue eyes when he opened the door.

"They got work for me back at the tugs. We're gonna move away from here and start over. Get us a house in Brooklyn. Things are lookin' up."

Brooklyn and Back

Things did look up for a while. The duplex on East Forty-seventh Street even had a yard. Not big enough to put a picnic table in, but still, it *was* a yard. Jim could walk to Bergen Beach and go swimming. He missed his friends from Harlem—Bull McDermott, Hammerhead Riley, Pete Darogoth—but there'd be new friends here, like all the other places.

Erasmus High School impressed Jim more than any school he'd ever been to. But after changing school fifteen times in eleven years, he couldn't keep up with the work. He felt as if something valuable had been taken away from him as he viewed the enthusiasm with which the other students did their work. *They* would succeed. Proudly clutching their neatly rolled diplomas, they would march on to respectable jobs, houses with neat white fences, children who sang in the choir. But Jim? Oh, he'd march too—but not on the same road. He'd move forever from job to job, tenement to tenement, slum to slum, always looking for something better. The thought wouldn't leave him alone. It lingered in the shadows of his mind, seeking to darken any small glimmers of hope that entered there.

They didn't stay on East Forty-seventh Street long. After about a year and a half they moved again—this time to a house near Coney Island. One day while scanning the Coney Island Amusement Park for dropped nickels, Jim thought about something he had heard many times from his mother's lips. "Why should you be a burden on him? He's not your real father anyway. I guess you're just too scared to run away!" Too scared? A sudden bravado swelled his chest. He wasn't too scared. He picked up a shining object, but found it was only a discarded gum wrapper. He flicked it downward, setting his mouth in a firm line. He'd show them who was too scared.

NOBODY'S BOY

Scared, huh? What was there to be scared of? Nothing could be worse than the feelings of frustration, guilt, and defeat he got around them.

He arrived at East Forty-seventh Street around nightfall. The lights in Skip's house cast a yellowish glow on the sidewalk in front. Skip's room was dark, so Jim waited. If he could just bide his time till the light went on, he'd be OK. Skip would help him out. He always had before. He sat on the ground, leaning against a garbage can, his eye on Skip's window. It seemed as if hours had passed when finally a dim yellow glow revealed a figure walking across the room. Jim stood up. Yeah, it was Skip, all right. He clenched the bottle cap tightly in his hand a moment, then flung it upward toward the second-floor window.

He heard the window opening, then saw Skip's curly black head pop out.

"Well, whaddaya know! What brings you back to your old neighborhood, Jim?"

Jim fought back a smile and whispered into the darkness in mock anger.

"Whaddaya wanna do? Tell the whole neighborhood. Come on down here and help me out."

The window had barely been slammed shut before a lanky figure appeared beside the garbage can. Skip surveyed the small bundle of clothes tied to Jim's belt.

"Hey, man, looks to me like you ain't aimin' on goin' back home for a while."

"I can't take it anymore, Skip. They don't want me. You know that. They never did. I'm not lookin' for no pity. Just a place to stay."

"I got an idea." Skip's eyes brightened. This was going to be fun—sneaking, plotting, putting one over on the old lady. "You can stay in the attic. I'll sneak your meals up. Maybe you could even get a job. They're lookin' for help in the grocery store."

Fear and relief flooded through Jim at the same time. He'd made it this far. He had a place to stay; Skip was helping him out. But how long would it work?

A week later Jim sauntered down East Forty-seventh Street, hands in pockets, whistling a tune. He hadn't expected the plan

BROOKLYN AND BACK

to go so well. Maybe Skip's mother knew, but she never let on. The job at the grocery store had worked out, and to prove it he had on a new blue shirt and unpatched pants—the first purchases from his *own* paycheck. Jim lifted his head proudly and looked down the street to see whether anyone was watching him. Then he saw it. The familiar old black car looked like it could hardly go another block. The boy wanted to run, but he was rooted to the spot, and running was useless anyway. Just as the car pulled up alongside him, a loud pop sounded and the right tire began hissing its way down to the rim. David Finley yanked the jack out of the back seat and slammed the door, cursing loudly. Then he spotted Jim.

"So this is where you been hiding out. Well, the only reason I came to get ya is 'cause of your mother. I don't care if you *never* come home!" Four-year-old John stood behind his father, hands on hips, his little mouth twisted into the typical expression he had become so accustomed to in his short life.

"Where'd ya get the clothes, Bub?"

Jim tried to ignore him. The jack kept slipping, and his stepfather was having a hard time.

"Need some help, Dad?" It took a lot to say it, but he tried to think of the times his stepfather had helped him out.

"No, I don't need any of your help. You're nothin' to me. Ya hear that, boy? Nothin'. And I don't *ever* need *your* help."

Jim picked up an empty can, squashed it in his hands, and threw it to the ground. He was glad his stepfather had said that. It meant he wouldn't have to go home with him. He didn't need the man anyway. He turned on his heel and stalked angrily down the street, followed by John, who impatiently queried, "Where'd ya get the clothes, Bub?"

That night Jim met some of his friends at the square. Just as they were trying to decide what to do for excitement, a police car pulled up, lights flashing. Behind it sputtered an old black jalopy. A burly officer jumped out of the cruiser and demanded, "All right, which one of you is James Finley?"

Before anyone could answer, David Finley was out of his car, grabbing Jim by the collar.

"This is the kid, officer." Then turning on Jim, he raised his

27

NOBODY'S BOY

voice to an angry yell. "Now, let me tell you one thing, boy, if you don't get in that car *now*, I'll put you in reform school till you're 21."

Jim's cool eyes met his stepfather's angry ones squarely. "Good. I'd rather be in reform school than home with you."

If his words had hurt David Finley, as Jim intended, the man's face showed no indication of it. He merely opened the door of the car and pushed Jim roughly into the back seat. In all the excitement, Beulah, who was occupying the front seat, fainted. But as soon as they were out of the policemen's sight she revived, her voice as strong as ever.

"James, you're enough to drive a mother crazy. You think you can just walk in or walk out whenever you feel like it. You don't care about anybody but yourself. Well, it's about time you learned a little respect." She turned and glared at him in disgust. "When we get home, you head for your room and stay there. You're going to learn to do as you're told and straighten up!"

Jim leaned back in the seat, a new plan formulating in his mind. Every once in a while a word or phrase jumped out at him from his mother's endless droning " . . . troublesome . . . always a bother . . . such a worry . . . " He concentrated harder, blocking out the cutting words. He had to think of a better plan this time. He had to go farther. If it hadn't been for those truant officers, his parents never would have come looking for him anyway. They didn't really want him. The whole scene had just been an act for the benefit of the law.

The car lurched to a stop, and Jim looked dully out the window. Home was no welcome relief.

For the next few months Jim bided his time. When fall came, he entered his fourth year at Lafayette High School. One day in late September, David Finley announced that he would be out on the tugs for a month. He spoke few words to Jim before going. "I don't want you to be leaving your mother alone while I'm not here. She's a sick woman, and if I find out you've been out of the house while she's home alone, I'll give it to you when I get back." Jim nodded, catching his father's true intent and knowing that his mother would make it difficult for him to carry out the assignment. At first he tried to stay home as much as he

28

BROOKLYN AND BACK

could. But he tired of the impatient looks and scolding words that came whenever he stayed around the house too long.

David Finley came home unexpectedly one evening in late October to find Jim gone. When his stepson finally arrived, he greeted him with venomous words. "I thought I told you to stay home with your mother, boy! Well, I ain't puttin' up with you no longer." In the midst of the beating that followed, Jim resolved that he, too, would put up with it no longer.

The next afternoon he grabbed the back of a trolley car and rode the length of Brooklyn, crossing the Brooklyn Bridge into Manhattan. From there he sneaked onto a ferry to New Jersey. Arriving at Jersey City, Jim approached the car barn. A balding man in faded blue pants eyed him quizzically. "You lookin' for somebody, boy?" Jim tried not to sound too anxious. "Yeah. I'm looking for my stepbrother. His name's Dave Finley and he drives the trolley for public service." The man scratched his head, while Jim fought to organize his despairing thoughts into an alternate plan. If only he'd thought to get Dave's address.

"Dave Finley, you say?" The stranger's voice interrupted Jim's thoughts. "He works at the Union City car barn. 'Bout four miles from here."

Every step of those four miles jarred another question into Jim's troubled mind. What would Dave and Lilly say? Would they send him back? And if he were sent back, what would they do to him this time? What was reform school like? Could anything be worse than life as it was now?

The sign hanging precariously from a dingy post announced the Union City car barn. Jim entered the weathered building and found a man in round spectacles writing busily behind a counter. "Excuse me," Jim began in an attempt to arrest the man's attention. "I'm looking for Dave Finley." Getting no reply, he added, "I'm wondering if you could help me?" The man continued writing. Then sounding very disturbed, he suddenly snarled out three words: "He already left."

"He lives on Garvin Avenue, kid. 48B Garvin Avenue. It's just a couple blocks from here." The voice came from a red-headed boy about Jim's age, who was sweeping the floor. Jim reacted to this uncommon courtesy with grateful surprise.

29

NOBODY'S BOY

"Hey, thanks a lot. See ya around."

When he knocked on the door of the red brick apartment, Dave opened the door. He did not appear to be greatly surprised.

"Well, Jim, Lilly and I've been waiting for you for a couple of years now. How'd you ever stand it for so long?"

In the weeks that followed, Jim found himself becoming absorbed into his stepbrother's household, which included Dave's two children by a previous marriage, Lilly's blind father, and a vicious red chow dog. Dave paid Jim one dollar a week to cook all the meals, bathe the blind man, and help around the house. Jim knew his stepbrother was using him, but it gave him a means of escape from home, and he didn't complain. The truant officers couldn't bother him as long as he stayed in New Jersey, where State laws permitted teen-agers to drop out of school at the age of 16, one year younger than New York State allowed.

As the days and weeks went by, Jim found himself spending more time with Pop Morrison, Lilly's father. The two became bonded together by the common realization that they existed only as a burden to others.

Jim had tried to escape, but Pop was too old to protest. His grandchildren laughed at him, cruelly mocking his slow walk, feeble voice, and groping blindness. Dave took his pension; Lilly sighed at his helplessness.

The old man told Jim everything: how he became blind, how to cook a chicken, how to wrap his ankle in twine and break an egg on it when he sprained it. Together they planned to run away someday, to shed forever the shackles of living with people who didn't want them.

Six months after moving in with Dave and Lilly, Jim turned 17. He had looked forward to this day ever since he could remember. He was legally free in any State. Pop Morrison understood. After all, he couldn't expect Jim to stick around and keep an old man company until he died. Placing a hand on Jim's shoulder, he hoarsely whispered into the boy's ear: "Them plans ain't ruined yet, Jim. At least one of us is gonna make it."

Coney Island Behind

On the trolley car to Coney Island, Jim thought about his mother and stepfather. He didn't care about seeing them again, didn't want to go home, but it seemed to be the best plan temporarily. He didn't know what he would do, but he wanted to get a job and earn more money than the dollar a week Dave had been giving him.

Climbing the steps to the Coney Island apartment, Jim cast an apprehensive glance at the door he knew so well. He hesitated a minute, surveying the cracked, peeling brown paint, listening to the familiar querulous voices inside. Then he knocked.

He put his hands in his pockets and leaned against a post as someone unbolted the door. David Finley swung it open and stood facing his stepson, a smile forming on his thin lips. He hitched up his pants, then thrust out his right hand.

"Well, boy, don't just stand there! Come in! Come in!" He pulled his stepson into the apartment, then turned toward the back bedroom.

"Beulah, Beulah! It's the boy. He's come back. Git out here and welcome your son home!"

His mother's heavy figure appeared at the doorway, a lock of brown hair hanging limply over her wide forehead. When she saw Jim, a grin split her pudgy face, and the sugary, meaningless words began to flow.

"James, I just knew you'd be back. You couldn't stay away from your loving mother forever, now could you? I knew the day you left that you'd be back. Why, I told your father just yesterday that now that the holidays are here you'd be coming home, looking to the only folks who've ever cared anything about you."

NOBODY'S BOY

She pulled him to her stout body, fleshy arms enfolding him, endless voice droning on.

"Now, let's see. This calls for a celebration. I'll start boiling up some potatoes and fix 'em how you like 'em . . ."

Jim freed himself and slumped to the couch. In his mind he heard the same voice seven years before, promising and alluring, sweet and thick, coating the cheap words that provided no love. He'd wanted to go back to Uncle Harold then. This time he thought not of running back, but of bolting ahead, of fleeing through the paint-peeled door to brighter entries, glassy and new, opening into worlds of adventure.

The March day dawned bright and clear as Jim smoothed his coat and walked out the door of the Finleys' Coney Island apartment. He was headed for the postal telegraph, where he'd been working for the past three and one-half months. Halfway down the hall, he turned and called, "I might be late, Ma. I'm stoppin' in to talk with the Navy recruiters on Flatbush Avenue, so I don't know when I'll be home."

Later, as Jim sat waiting his turn outside the recruiting office he turned his mind to his home life. The celebration of his return hadn't lasted long, he thought, recalling the bitter words and angry looks that had punctuated his months at home. *Well, if only I can get into the Navy, I won't be a trouble to anybody again.*

"Next, please."

Jim looked up quickly, then self-consciously followed the officer into the adjoining room. After his physical, a nurse, whose pixie face was framed by a fluff of light hair, pushed some forms in his direction.

"All set," she smiled. "Now just have your father sign these forms and bring them back in as soon as you can." She turned her attention to the still-seated applicants. "Next?"

Trudging home, Jim gripped the forms and pondered his new problem. "*Just* have your father sign the forms," she had said. Easy for her to say. David Finley was on the tugs, stuck in the ice somewhere around Albany. Why, he might have to wait a whole month before his father could sign the forms. And then there'd be another wait . . . The disturbing thoughts went on until

32

CONEY ISLAND BEHIND

he reached the apartment. Yanking open the battered door, he threw himself onto the sagging couch.

Beulah eyed her son in mock pity. "I knew they'd never take you, James. They don't want people in the Navy with one lung. And besides, there's plenty of other reasons you couldn't pass the physical."

"I *passed* the physical!" Jim exploded. "And I've got *two* lungs. The only trouble is that my father's supposed to sign the papers and where's my old man? Stuck in the ice in Albany!"

Beulah's expression changed instantly. Immediately she grabbed her pocketbook and headed for the door.

"Where are *you* going, Ma?"

"You want those papers signed, don't you? If I can get to a phone booth in time, I can probably catch your brother Dave at work. His signature should set you free, since you don't seem to want to stay around your poor mother any longer."

She slammed the door, leaving Jim slouched on the couch, wondering whether Dave's signature could really free him.

One week later Jim sat by the window of a train headed for boot camp in Norfolk, Virginia.

The next few weeks passed rapidly. The marching, drilling, and regulations were not easy, but it was better than home. For the first time in his life Jim put himself entirely into something. He had a purpose, a goal. He was training, with others, to serve his country in the United States Navy.

The busy days of boot camp passed quickly. When the basic training was over, Jim was assigned to a Navy machinist school. This was different from the other schools he'd been going to all his life. Everybody started fresh here. Nobody had the edge on him this time.

Jim had always enjoyed tinkering with machines, and he caught onto his new trade rapidly. Eagerly he assimilated the facts and concepts, putting them to use as he worked on different machines.

One day John McGrorie, a sailor from the Bronx, persuaded Jim to box for their platoon. Jim hadn't done much in the pugilistic line lately; he hadn't even gotten into a fight in several months. But John was convincing.

33

NOBODY'S BOY

"Come on, Jim. You'll be a champ in no time. You ain't a real big guy, but you're fast on your feet. You'll dance your opponent right into a corner before he even knows what happened. Come on, Jim, you'll do it for the platoon, won't ya?"

Jim had nodded unenthusiastically. Then, thinking of the time he'd taken care of the kid who threw Donald Miller's ball over the roof, he warmed to the project. Sure, he'd do it. He'd just put up his fists and the guy would be out cold.

At the first-round bell, Jim bounded out of his corner, pleasantly conscious of the shouts of the excited crowd.

"Come on, Jimmy! Give it to 'im!"

But his ring-wise opponent raised a muscled arm and smashed his knotty fist into Jim's rapidly approaching nose. With the blood gushing down his face, Jim slumped to the floor.

"... eight ... nine ... ten! And the winner is ... Joe Pulaski!"

Back in the barracks some of the guys in the platoon tried to cheer up the defeated boxer, but their words had little effect. Knocked out in the first round! This would be the last time he'd ever let himself get flattered into a boxing ring!

In the months that followed, Jim became increasingly independent. He went home on leave occasionally, but not as the 17-year-old boy who had left home on that windy March day, gripping the papers that held the key to his freedom. Things were different now. He was 19 and had been in the service for almost two years. He did what he wanted to do: stayed out late, went to bars, barely listened to or even noticed his badgering parents.

After machinist school, Jim waited with others to be transferred. The Navy ships took a few men every day, and the platoon shrank as the men were assigned to the *Wasp, Ranger, Hornet, Yorktown,* and others. The old crowd dwindled, but still Jim remained.

One day as he was napping, Jim felt a rough hand on his shoulder. A dark, burly man was speaking quietly in a thick German accent.

"I haf here fife transfers for machinists. They vill go to New London, Connecticut. For tventy-fife dollars you can be vun.

CONEY ISLAND BEHIND

Are you interested?"

Jim blinked his eyes rapidly, thoughts spinning in his head. New London, Connecticut? Where was that? Oh, well, what did he have to lose? He had to go somewhere, and it might as well be wherever-it-was in Connecticut.

"I'll take it," he said quickly. Little did James Finley know that this simple assent would ultimately lead him on a journey so miraculous that in time he would see it as the turning point in his life.

New London and West

In New London, Jim settled into his life with growing confidence. By day he worked at Machine Shop 31, making parts to repair submarines. Nights he went out with his friends, seeking such entertainment as the small seacoast town had to offer.

Bob Ryan, an old friend from Harlem, was also stationed in New London. Often the two self-assured young sailors swaggered along the streets at night, whistling jovially. One such night they found themselves several miles from the submarine base, and Ryan decided he felt too tired to walk back. He eyed a shiny black Hudson parked on the side of the road, keys dangling temptingly in the ignition.

Quickly he crossed to the driver's side. Without even turning around he called to Jim, "C'mon, Finley. Whaddya waitin' for? Here's our taxi parked right here just for us."

Jim hesitated, making sure no one was in sight. Then he climbed into the front seat, just as his buddy started the motor. Ryan laughed a little nervously. "It's not like we're stealing a car or anything, see? I just didn't feel like walkin' back, and since somebody was kind enough to let us borrow his car, we couldn't refuse him, now could we?"

Jim grinned and shook his head vigorously. "We sure wouldn't want to hurt the man's feelings, seein' as he offered."

Laughing at their own joke, the two sailors drove the "borrowed" car back to the sub base and left it in the parking lot.

When several days passed and no one mentioned anything about a stolen car, Jim and Ryan decided their plan had been successful. After that, whenever they tired of walking, or needed to get somewhere in a hurry, they always managed to find a car just waiting to be "borrowed."

NEW LONDON AND WEST

Jim and Ryan "borrowed" their last car on Christmas Eve, 1941. Snow swirled around the old green Studebaker as the two Navy men headed for the train depot, eagerly discussing the coming holiday. At the station they jumped out of the car and gathered up their baggage. Neither one noticed the small piece of white paper that fell to the floor of the Studebaker as Bob Ryan struggled to get his suitcase from the back seat.

As soon as Ryan returned from New York, he was summoned to the police station and informed that detectives searching a stolen car had found an allotment paper made out in his name. A sharp young officer told him that his case was open and shut and that he would be sentenced in two weeks. Ryan would await the decision in jail.

When Jim heard the news, all of his newly acquired self-confidence drained out of him. Ryan had been caught! Sooner or later they'd know he'd been in on it too. And then what? Jim sat down heavily on his bunk, kicking aside his newly shined boots. Well, it had been nice while it lasted. For a while he'd actually thought he might make it. Thought he might actually *learn* something, *do* something, *be* somebody. But, no. Even the Navy couldn't straighten him out.

That night Jim tried to fight off his agitated thoughts, but his mind whirled on, torturing him with voices from the past: "Whitey, you're the one that made my boy bad." "Your father never wanted you anyway." "I don't care if you *never* come home."

As the first rays of light penetrated the cracks in his blinds, Jim fell into an uneasy sleep and dreamed of houses with neat white fences, children singing in a church choir, families laughing together. But always he was on the outside, separated from them by a transparent wall too high for him to climb. He banged on the glass, but no one could hear him. And so he kept walking, walking through the dream world until he thought he would drop, going nowhere yet unable to stop.

Jim awoke with a queasy feeling in the pit of his stomach. He waited out the next two weeks with fear constantly nagging at his thoughts. He visited Ryan every day, bringing him cakes and pies and begging him not to tell.

37

NOBODY'S BOY

He was walking to the mess hall one day when a sailor finally brought him the news. "Did ya hear they decided Ryan's case today? He got a bad conduct discharge." Jim felt his heart stop, as he waited, but the sailor had finished talking.

"Anything else? I mean . . . was there anybody else involved?" Jim knew he had sounded too obvious.

"Anybody else? No. Why? You know something I don't?"

"Just wonderin'. Ryan must've thought he was smart tryin' to pull something like that on his own." Jim turned the corner and hastened his step, relief flooding through him.

By that evening, Jim was himself again. Whistling, he stepped jauntily along, heading for the annual sub base Valentine dance. Once inside the crowded hall, he leaned against the wall, looking over the girls. Many of them attended sub base events frequently, and they talked and laughed with ease as various sailors escorted them around. Elbowing his way through the crowd, Jim spotted a sparkling blonde.

"Hey, Katherine, happy Valentine's Day!" he said with a grin.

"Oh, hi, Jim." Katherine tossed back her golden mane and flashed him a bright smile. "I'd like to introduce you to a few friends of mine. This is Linda [she gestured toward a tall redhead], and Theresa [she pointed to a shorter girl in a bright-red gown], and Gloria Jackson." Gloria smiled self-consciously, pushing back a wisp of dark-brown hair.

"Glad to meet all of you. Where are you from, Gloria?" Jim focused his attention on the slender young woman.

"I live in Greeneville." Gloria's quiet voice contrasted with the loud laughter and pretentious chatter on all sides. "I've lived in New England all my life."

Lived in New England all her life. He pondered it as the chilly February winds nipped at his cheeks on the way back to the barracks. Had she moved around from one New England town to the next, as he had moved from street to street in New York City? Or could she trace her past back to two or three neatly painted houses in quiet neighborhoods? He was still thinking about it as he dialed the telephone the next evening.

"Hello?" Her quiet voice interrupted his thoughts.

38

NEW LONDON AND WEST

"Gloria?"

"Yes."

"This is Jim Finley." He waited for some sign of recognition, then continued. "I've got a friend that's having a party next Saturday night over on Ocean Avenue. If you wanna meet me there, we can hang around at the party for a while and then come over to the dance at the sub base."

She didn't answer right away, so he went on. "The party is supposed to start about eight. It's the white house beside the pharmacy on Ocean Avenue. Sorry I can't pick you up, but I don't have a car and I've had enough of borrowed cars." He laughed nervously.

"What's so funny?"

"Oh, nothin'—private joke. Maybe I'll tell you about it someday, if I get to know you well enough."

"I guess I can make it Saturday night," she replied, ignoring his comment.

"Good. Well, I don't wanna waste your time talkin' on the phone all evening, so I'll see ya then."

"'Bye."

"See ya later." He placed the receiver on the hook and headed for his room, grinning.

Jim didn't have much time to think about Saturday night during the next few days, as Machine Shop 31 had received several rush orders. Each morning he dragged himself out of bed at five o'clock to go into work, and did not return to the barracks until nine or ten at night.

By the time Saturday came, Jim was wracked with doubts about his date with Gloria. He'd worked hard all week and didn't feel up to trying to impress anybody. He needed a break. Gloria barely knew him and she'd get over it if he didn't show up. He'd hitchhike to the bar and have a couple of drinks.

Jim stuck out his thumb in front of the barracks, backing slowly along the road as the car headlights flashed past him. After about ten cars whizzed by, a Chevy full of girls pulled over. Jim raced to the car and opened the door. A gasp from the front seat attracted his attention. Then he saw her.

"Gloria Jackson! Just what do you think you're doing in this

NOBODY'S BOY

car heading in the *opposite* direction from Ocean Avenue? How dare you actually try to stand me up?"

"Me? It doesn't look like *you* were heading that way either, sailor." Her voice didn't sound as soft as he had remembered it.

They stared angrily at each other for a few moments, until the other girls began to get impatient. "Look, why don't you just hop in and we can all get going to the dance?" The driver flashed Jim an annoyed look.

Jim climbed in beside Gloria and slammed the door. He sat in silence while the girls chatted excitedly about the dance, seemingly forgetting the embarrassing incident. When the driver finally pulled the car into a parking space, Jim's anger had dissipated and he couldn't keep quiet any longer.

"You know, Gloria, someday we're gonna laugh about this."

Cold February winds blew icy bits of snow against their faces as they stepped out of the car and walked toward the brightly lit building. Jim decided he was actually glad for the strange turn of events and took Gloria by the hand. "I really mean that, Gloria. Someday we'll be laughing about this and nobody will ever believe us when we tell the story."

Later that evening, Mrs. Jackson did laugh with her daughter over the strange coincidence. But then Gloria became serious.

"I could never marry anybody like Jim, Mother. He's so crazy—always laughing and joking. The only reason I'm dating him is because it's wartime. I don't want to go out with someone seriously and then get my heart broken when he goes to sea or something."

The conversation came back to Gloria a year later as she sat across the table from Jim in the Pirate's Den. It all seemed so long ago; funny how emotions could change almost imperceptibly. But Jim's voice interrupted her musings.

"Hey, you really like to keep a guy in suspense, don't you?"

She laughed, her blue eyes softening. "Oh, of course I'll marry you! What do you think I am—one of those girls that just dates any old guy during wartime so her heart won't be broken?"

The wedding took place eleven months later, on a sleety

NEW LONDON AND WEST

January day. Jim called Gloria on a Friday with the news that they could go ahead and get married. His ten-day leave had been approved. The following Monday they stood before the priest in the rectory, Jim in his best Navy blues, Gloria in the burgundy dress she'd been saving for so long. Her sister stood beside her as the maid of honor, her uncle as the best man.

Jim squeezed her hand tightly as the priest rapidly flipped through the pages of a small black book, found his place, and looked up. "Before we begin this service, I must be sure of one thing." He directed his comments to Jim.

"Do you promise to bring your children up in the Catholic faith?"

"Yes, I do." It was an easy promise to make. Even though Jim had been brought up Protestant, he'd never cared too much about religion, and he respected Gloria for her strong beliefs. Sure, he'd bring his children up Catholic. They'd be just like Gloria; nothing wrong with that—that'd be something to be proud of.

As they rode the train to New York on their honeymoon, Jim shared some of these thoughts with his new wife. "Ya know, I really think it's good the way you go to church every week and all." He studied the floor for a minute, noting the shine on his rounded black shoes, the dainty pointed toes on Gloria's brown ones. "Sometimes I feel like there's something missing in my life. Once when I was a kid I jumped up on this crazy soapbox right out on the street and preached my heart out. Funny, I can't remember what got into me, but I felt like going home and telling the whole neighborhood." He glanced sideways, trying to read her thoughts. "You probably think I sound crazy or something."

She shook her head, watching the gray clouds breaking up outside the narrow window of the speeding train.

He continued. "It's just that someday I'm gonna find out what life's really all about—and not just on the surface. I mean way down deep, where it all counts."

Gloria thought about those words often during the early weeks of marriage. She'd always seen Jim as so sure of himself, so ready to laugh, so eager to conquer the world. She was only just beginning to glimpse the sensitivity hidden behind his

41

NOBODY'S BOY

light-blue eyes.

They'd been married a month when she returned home from work one day to find his packed sea bag hidden behind the closet door and turned to face those blue eyes, heavy with the weight of swollen lids.

"You weren't supposed to see it," he began. "I wanted to tell you first. They just transferred me today. They'll let you come out as soon as I get settled. We've got until tomorrow."

The next morning she watched his waving hand till the train moved out of sight, carrying him to California.

Mare Island and Holding

The days passed slowly for Gloria, brightened only by the letters from California that came so frequently. But one windy Saturday she returned empty-handed from the mailbox, and disappointment welled up within her. Mrs. Jackson met her at the door. "Jimmy's mother's on the phone, Gloria." She looked at her daughter with concern. "She wants to talk to you right away."

Gloria felt her heart pounding as she hurried through the doorway and into the kitchen.

"Hello?" She fumbled nervously with the cord.

"Well, have you been notified yet?" Beulah sounded hoarse. "Jim's dead. Killed in an explosion. Happened this morning."

Gloria managed to find a chair and sat down. Her hands no longer fumbled with the telephone cord. She couldn't move; couldn't talk. She stared straight ahead, trying to focus on the fading roses on the wallpaper.

"Gloria?" Beulah's voice startled her. "Just thought somebody ought to let you know. And . . . " She broke into loud sobs, unable to continue.

"Thank you." Gloria finally focused on the roses. "And goodbye." Methodically she arose, placed the receiver on the hook, then sat down at the table again. Praying silently, she cleared her muddy thoughts only long enough to assure herself of one thing—Jim was not dead. He had to be alive. There was some mistake.

"Gloria, are you all right?" Mrs. Jackson's shoes tapped echoes across the kitchen floor.

"Yes, Mother, I'm all right. And so is Jim. He's *not* dead. I know he's not dead." Gloria picked up the receiver again and

43

NOBODY'S BOY

dialed the number she had taped to the phone. She concentrated on counting the rings. When a voice finally answered, she stated her business calmly, matter-of-factly, without stumbling over her words.

"This is Gloria Finley in Connecticut. My husband, James, is stationed at the Mare Island Navy Yard. I've just received unofficial word that he was killed in an explosion this morning." She stopped for a moment, took a deep, ragged breath, then went on. "I'm calling to find out if it's true."

She was glad when she'd finished talking. She didn't like saying the words, admitting even the slightest possibility that this horror could possibly be reality.

"Could you hold the line, please, ma'am? This is going to require some checking." The voice was businesslike.

The interminable waiting began, the checking and rechecking, the ever-widening gap between the known and unknown. Behind her, the familiar kitchen clock lightly clicked away the seconds as Gloria waited. She alternately listened to its lulling tempo and the occasional mysterious clicks of the telephone in her hand.

Long after the thousandth second had punctuated the silence, the nameless voice on the other end spoke.

"Mrs. Finley?" The flat voice gave no indication of the news to come.

"Yes?"

"There have been two explosions. But we have no information yet about who was involved. As soon as we receive word . . ."

Gloria turned and looked dully out the window, only faintly aware of the voice on the other end of the line now. Moments later she became conscious of the endless droning of the phone and wondered how long it had been since he'd hung up.

Then she spoke. "Well, Mother, I guess the best thing to do is keep busy. This floor could use a good washing anyway."

She concentrated on the suds bubbling up as she filled the bucket with water. She scrubbed one section of the floor at a time, watching the soapy rivulets swirl around the patterned linoleum. As she finally dumped the last bucket of dirty water out

44

MARE ISLAND AND HOLDING

the back door, she heard the phone ring.

As if in a daze, she strained to hear her mother's voice. It seemed unusually loud.

"No. No, we haven't heard anything yet . . ."

Gloria stepped away from the door and squeezed out her mop. Before going in, she inhaled the cold winter air deeply. She stood quietly for a minute, praying for strength and watching the sun's last rays stretch across the sky. Then she realized that the concrete steps were cold beneath her slippered feet, and she turned and opened the door.

Her mother had just hung up the phone. "That was your father. Said he'd be here in about an hour." She placed her arm about her daughter's rigid shoulders. "Why don't we cook up a stew or something?"

Glad for the chance to keep occupied, Gloria began peeling carrots. By the time her father arrived, a tired calmness had replaced the dull ache in her body. The hot stew seemed to soothe and relax her. After clearing away the dishes, she sat knitting while her mother and father talked quietly in the living room.

By ten o'clock Gloria realized the phone was not going to ring, so she said her prayers and went to bed. She awoke only twice during the night; each time, she prayed for courage and quickly fell asleep again. The next morning, as she dressed for mass, the phone rang. She threw on a robe and hurried for the kitchen.

"Hello?" She didn't bother to sit down.

"Gloria? This is Jim. How ya doin'?"

She pulled out a chair, and for the first time since the ordeal began, she felt hot tears on her cheeks.

"Hey, don't ya remember me anymore? Some reaction a guy gets from his wife. Calls her up and she won't even talk to him. And here I was calling to let you know it's all set for you to come out to California."

Then he realized that she was crying.

"What's the matter, honey? What's wrong?"

Gloria swallowed hard, struggling for words. "I *knew* you were alive," she finally managed to say.

NOBODY'S BOY

Gloria leaned back, enjoying the warmth of the early-morning April sun that streamed through the train window, watching through half-closed eyes as last-minute passengers scrambled for their seats. A heavy woman in a dark-blue dress sat down beside her, and immediately her thoughts turned to Beulah. She held no contempt for her mother-in-law, only pity for a woman whose life was so miserable that she sought to make others unhappy too.

But Gloria didn't let her thoughts stay on Beulah for long. True, she'd been through a lot the day of that phone call, but that was in the past. Jim was alive, and they'd be together again in another five hours.

Gloria straightened up and looked out the window at the passing shades of green. Her three and one-half days of traveling all blurred into one, but the five hours ahead seemed endless.

When she finally stepped off the train in California, Gloria felt as though she had entered a new world. Mild, moist breezes soothed the aches imposed on her by the train trip; green hills sloping down to the ocean awakened a feeling of freshness she hadn't experienced in a long time. In the midst of it all stood Jim, sailor hat just a little too far back on his head, blue eyes smiling.

They resumed their life together as if there had been no three-month interruption, yet with a sweetness unique to their marriage. Jim worked on machines in the Mare Island Navy Yard and Gloria got a job in the payroll department. They rented a room, stayed up late, sipping chocolate and building dreams, and counted themselves lucky to be alive and together.

It was almost perfect, but not quite. Something was still missing. Jim tried to put it into words one morning as Gloria poured the orange juice for breakfast.

"I've been thinking a lot about the direction of our lives lately. We might not have a whole lot of money, but we're happy—we've got a nice life together. Yet, still sometimes I wonder, Isn't there something more?"

Gloria looked across the table at her husband and marked his expression. He was so young, so eager to answer all the questions life threw his way.

MARE ISLAND AND HOLDING

"Why don't you come to church with me?" she suggested simply.

For a year he tried it. He sat through mass, read an old catechism, thought about deeper issues. And there were times he felt close to understanding, times he thought he might find the something that was lacking, but always it evaded him, always it kept him wondering.

One evening as he and Gloria were eating dinner, she brought up a subject that was to be the key to all his musings.

"I've been wondering about something, Jim," she began. "In making out the payroll at work I've noticed that a certain group of men never come in on Saturday. Yet they make up the time every Sunday. Why do you think that is?"

Jim passed it off lightly. "I don't know—could be something to do with some kind of religion."

It would be years before he would understand.

47

San Diego and Onward

The July heat beat down upon the two sailors as yet another car whizzed past them. "It's useless. Nobody's gonna pick us up." Dark-haired Ed Gimbel wiped the sweat from his forehead. "We've gotta find a car, Jim, or we'll never get to Napa."

Jim nodded and sat down on the side of the road. "I'm beat, Ed. Let's rest awhile, then try that parking lot about a quarter of a mile from here." He leaned his head against a tree and closed his eyes. Immediately Gloria danced into his brain.

It had been three months since she'd gotten on the train to head back for the East Coast. Jim pulled idly at a long piece of grass and considered the situation. Three thousand miles was a long way. But they'd decided it would be best. After all, their tiny apartment in the worst end of the city was no place for a baby. No, it was better this way. Gloria's mother could help out, and Gloria wouldn't have to worry about working or anything. He'd be out of the Navy soon enough.

"Hey, don't get too comfortable! We'd better get movin' if we ever expect to get there." Ed was starting down the road, mopping at the back of his neck with an already-moist handkerchief. Jim snapped a small twig in two, threw both pieces to the ground, and hurried to catch up.

Ed took large strides, anxious to get the walking over with, and Jim tried to match him. They arrived at the parking lot exhausted and hot. Strolling casually down the rows of cars, the two sailors spotted what they were looking for—a set of keys lying on the seat. Ed quickly slid behind the wheel while Jim jumped in on the passenger's side.

"Hit it, Ed, before anybody notices." The car was rolling out of the lot, and Jim looked anxiously toward the streams of

SAN DIEGO AND ONWARD

people going in and out of the nearby stores.

On the main road, Ed floored the gas pedal, and the quivering red speedometer needle edged toward ninety. Neither sailor saw the bend in the road until it was too late. Ed's foot groped desperately for the brake as the car flew upward, flipped over, and landed on its roof. With panic flooding his throat, Jim struggled to right himself. The back of his head throbbed, and warm blood trickled past his left eye. Tiny fragments of glass stung his cheek.

"Jim, are you all right? Come on, we gotta get outa here before the cops arrive." Ed's voice was slurred, but he inched his way through the jagged opening in the windshield, and Jim struggled to follow.

Once out of the car, Jim began wiping the blood off his face with a handkerchief. Ed eyed him closely. "You're OK, Jim. Gave you quite a scare, though, didn't it? Come on, let's get outa here." He led the way into a wooded area beside the road. Five minutes later the two, still disheveled, emerged on a six-lane highway. Ed stuck out his thumb and began slowly backing up.

An old Ford squealed to a stop before Jim even had a chance to ask where they were going.

"Where to, boys?" The driver stuck his head out the window.

"We gotta get to the nearest police station, sir." Ed's voice had shifted to his politest tone, while Jim looked at him in surprise. It wasn't like Ed to turn himself in.

"Looks like you two got yourselves banged up a little," the driver remarked as he swung out into the lane of traffic. The two sailors settled nervously into the back seat.

"Yeah, that's why we gotta get to the police station. We were hitchhiking and some guys stopped, took our wallets, and beat us up," Ed answered.

Jim grinned in relief. Ed always managed to come up with something.

At the police station, two officers listened carefully to Ed's story. Bored with all the questions, Jim looked distractedly around the room. His head was beginning to throb again, and he was eager to leave. Just as he thought the ordeal was finished, a

NOBODY'S BOY

Shore Patrol officer strode into the room. "Found the car, all right. It was smashed up a couple miles from the parking lot. And this letter was on the front seat."

One of the policemen took a white envelope from the outstretched hand, and Jim suddenly felt sick. It was a letter he'd gotten from his mother that morning.

"The letter's addressed to a James Finley. Appears to be from his mother." The officer closest to Jim was scanning Beulah's barely legible handwriting. "Sounds like she's disowning him." He looked up with a sneer. "I guess you boys'll be spending the night."

Jim sat on the narrow cot staring at the cell walls. What would Gloria think? With each minute that ticked away, the relentless thoughts tortured him. He couldn't tell Gloria. She had so much faith in him. He hadn't pulled anything like this since they'd been married. She'd be shocked.

The next morning when the Navy lawyer came to take him to the district attorney in Napa, Jim felt almost overwhelmed with tiredness. His head throbbed from the accident and lack of sleep. Slowly he dragged himself to the waiting car.

In Napa, things went surprisingly well. The owner of the car had decided not to press charges. Jim and Ed were to pay $250 each for damages. That was all.

But somehow Jim couldn't share Ed's smiling relief. He stared at the blank sheet of paper on the table in front of him for more than an hour that night, unable to compose the letter. Finally, he managed the few lines.

Dear Gloria,

I have gotten myself into a bind and must have $250 as soon as possible. Please withdraw it from the account and send it out. I'll explain later.

I love you.

Jim.

The money arrived the following week. Two sentences of the accompanying letter stayed in Jim's mind as he went about his daily duties. "Jim, you don't have to worry about explaining why you need the money. I love and trust you enough to know it's important."

50

SAN DIEGO AND ONWARD

At times, Jim felt overwhelmed and humbled by Gloria's love for him. Never in his life had anyone had so much faith in him, cherished him so unconditionally.

He was thinking such thoughts as he repaired a machine at the Navy base one afternoon when the loudspeaker suddenly blared out his name, "James Finley. Long-distance telephone call. James Finley."

Jim rushed to the phone, wiping the grease from his hands as he ran. By the time he returned, breathless and elated, to his machine the word was out. James Finley had a son.

It was three months before Jim could get a home leave. Settling back in his train seat for the long ride, he reached into his pocket and drew out the picture Gloria had sent him of their son, Mark. He gazed with love at the turned-up nose and small, round face and thought of the promise the old priest had extracted two years before. The child would be reared a Catholic.

It had sounded so easy then. But would it be enough for this tiny baby when he had grown to be a man? Or would he, too, live balanced precariously on the edge of something, never quite arriving at that greater meaning toward which life so subtly hinted?

Arriving home four days later, Jim put aside these deeper questionings. He and Gloria talked for hours, trying to fill in the gap of the past six months in their six allotted days together. When he stepped onto the train again to return to California, Jim was certain of one thing—once out of the Navy, he would never again let a job or any other obligation keep him apart from Gloria.

Back in California, Jim was transferred from Mare Island to Albany. After working for four months repairing engines, he was moved once again, this time to San Diego, the beautiful seaport city of the south, with its world-famous salubrious climate.

One afternoon as he headed for a bar with his friend Bruno, an officious Shore Patrol officer appeared, seemingly from nowhere. "Square that hat, sailor!" came the command.

Jim stopped and made an elaborate adjustment to his

NOBODY'S BOY

headgear. Then, grinning at his pal, he moved on. But the SP, irritated and looking for trouble, followed. "Hey, Bruno," Jim questioned, laughing, "think I can scare him?" Then, turning, he shouted, "Boo!"

Suddenly five more SPs appeared. "Against the wall! Hands up!"

Bruno approached the first man truculently. "Hey, you can't do this to him. He ain't done nothin'!"

His words only infuriated the stocky man further. "You too! Against the wall!" In minutes the two friends were in a paddy wagon heading for jail.

The cell was communal, and was already peopled with drunken sailors. Several hours later Jim and Bruno learned of their offenses: "Disobeying authority, disturbing the peace, resisting arrest."

The next morning the two "criminals" began their manual labor—sweeping the streets of San Diego. But Bruno was just biding his time.

"That stinkin' SP ain't seen the end of me yet," he told Jim, and then broke into a torrent of obscenities over what he considered unfair treatment.

At the end of two weeks Jim was surprised to find that he would be released at the end of the day, but Bruno was put on an additional thirty-day restriction.

When Jim returned to the base, he found that the officers were looking for volunteers to go to Bikini Atoll in the Marshall Islands to take part in the testing of the atomic bomb. Still smarting because of the treatment he had received from the Shore Patrol and eager for a change, he decided to sign up.

Several weeks later Jim looked out on the sparkling Pacific from the flight deck of an aircraft carrier. Behind the ship followed an unwavering line of sharp black fins.

"Bet those sharks wouldn't mind if a man just happened to fall overboard," he remarked to a group of sailors.

Just then a droning voice came overhead. "Atten-tion!" an officer ordered. The men stood with their backs to Bikini as a bomber roared overhead. Then: "Drop to the floor. Heads down!"

SAN DIEGO AND ONWARD

A kaleidoscope of thoughts flickered rapidly through Jim's mind. He was glad to be on the flight deck rather than in the engine room. He'd have more of a chance, it seemed. He hoped Gloria wasn't too worried. He wondered whether Bruno was still pushing a broom down the streets of San Diego.

Suddenly the atmosphere became a searing flash of light accompanied by a tremendous blast. Jim kept his head down, but the engulfing brilliance infiltrated every corner of the deck, intruding even through the lids of his tightly closed eyes. He felt helplessly small, awed by the power that was beyond his understanding.

He experienced nearly the same feeling two weeks later when he learned that the *America Saratoga*, that mammoth ship that had seemed invincible through World War II, had been sunk in a test of atomic warfare on Naval vessels. Was man's scientific ingenuity the ultimate power? Jim scanned the horizon, but the endless expanse of blue offered no answer.

New England to Stay

Lingering rays of the September sun spread pastel patterns above the darkening Pacific as the *Saidor* eased into her berth. Jim hoisted his sea bag to his shoulders, intent on the silhouetted dock before him. It would be great to be on land again. A small crowd of welcoming people had gathered, their shadowed forms blended into a single shape.

The heavy vessel bumped against the weathered poles of the dock as the captain pulled up to moor. Two crew members sprang forward to let down the gangplank. Then sailors gathered up their belongings and began crossing to the dock.

Jim held back, letting those whose wives were waiting get off first. As his feet finally hit the pier, a big paw was thrust into his empty right hand.

"Welcome back, sailor!" Bruno pumped his hand, then slapped him jovially on the back several times. "You'll be glad to know I took care of that SP pal o' yours. Caught him in a bar without all his buddies to back him up. Gave it to him for both of us." A deep laugh rumbled from Bruno's throat as he recalled the incident. "Wish you coulda been there."

Jim pushed his hat farther back on his head, then ordered in mock seriousness, "Square that hat, sailor!" The two buddies laughed the whole length of the dock.

The next morning a sharp knock on the door awakened Jim from his first night's sleep on land in two months. "James Finley?" A tall sailor in Navy blues poked his head into the room. "You are to report to the officers' quarters at 0800."

Jim sat up on his cot and looked at his watch—six o'clock. No problem. "Yes, sir," he replied.

Two hours later, Jim sat outside an officer's door, wondering uneasily what kind of trouble he'd gotten himself into this time.

NEW ENGLAND TO STAY

Maybe the story of Bruno's fight had gotten out. Lucky thing he'd been out to sea. There'd be no way they could drag him into this one.

"James Finley, please."

Jim stood up and walked into the adjoining room. The transaction didn't take long.

"Your term of service is up shortly." The officer held up a paper from Jim's file. "Happy twenty-third birthday."

Jim reached out for the paper, his lips widening into a grin. Within a few weeks he'd be going home—home to the 1½-year-old son he'd barely even seen, home to Gloria.

They stood huddled together outside the train station as the November sky threw icy warnings of winter earthward. "Maybe that's your daddy's train now, Mark," Gloria told the light-haired boy in her brother-in-law's arms. Her sister Lucy checked her watch. "I think it is, Gloria; it's right on schedule."

Steel ground against steel as the train shivered to a stop. Passengers flowed into the raw weather, gripping suitcase handles and children's hands as they hurried toward shelter.

Gloria turned her attention from the train door for a moment to pick up one of Mark's red mittens. As she struggled to slip it back on her son's active little hand, she was suddenly whirled around. Jim caught her in a bear hug, dropping his sea bag beside them.

"Good thing I'm home," he murmured, brushing bits of frozen rain from her dark hair. "You would have turned into a pillar of ice if you'd waited out here much longer!"

Gloria laughed, kissing him, then reached for Mark. "Daddy's home, and we won't have to worry about him leaving us ever again." Jim grabbed his boy hungrily, holding the child tight against his rough Navy pea jacket.

Immediately Mark began to cry, "I want Mamma." He reached his red-mittened hands out to Gloria, and his shrieks grew more intense. "I want Mamma!"

"You're OK. Your daddy's got you."

"No. You're not my daddy! I want Mamma!" The child's voice grew louder.

NOBODY'S BOY

Gloria took the frightened boy into her arms, conscious of the curious looks of those passing by. Then her gloved hand caught Jim's, squeezing it tightly. "It'll take a little time," she whispered. "Just a little time."

Gray November days opened into the sun-bright whiteness of a crisp New England winter. As snowflakes fell silently outside the window, blending into a lush white blanket of security, so Jim built a relationship of trust with his son—gradually, patiently, consistently. Late afternoons, when Jim stamped the crusty snow off his workshoes, Mark opened the front door wide, releasing the home-warm smells of supper cooking and coffee bubbling. In the evening Jim sat on the couch with the small boy, the Sears catalog open between them. Pointing to each tool, Jim waited as Mark identified it with the name he had been taught: "Micrometer . . . caliper . . ." Gloria watched from the kitchen, a sense of contentment suffusing her as she sensed the common spark of determination between her Brooklyn-bred husband and this bright-eyed son. Jim had a good job with the Bostitch Company now, and things couldn't be better, she thought happily.

One afternoon, as the icicles dripped in response to an early spring, Gloria looked out the window and saw her parents leave their house across the street. They walked briskly, Mark Jackson holding a large package in both hands, Eva gripping his arm, a smile playing on her lips.

Gloria stepped out onto the porch to meet them. "You two sure look happy about something. Let me in on the secret."

Mark Jackson winked, then looked beyond his daughter to his namesake playing on the floor. "We've brought something special for somebody that lives here. Any little boys in this house?"

Mark was at his grandfather's side in an instant, focusing all attention on the parcel under his arm.

"A young fella came to our door selling these," the bearer of the mysterious package began, turning toward Gloria. "We thought it'd be nice if our grandson could have a set." He tore the brown wrapping from the outside, revealing a number of

NEW ENGLAND TO STAY

brightly colored books. Gloria inspected the top one, bending down to show it to Mark.

"The Bible Story, by Arthur S. Maxwell. Well, aren't these something! The pictures are beautiful!'' She looked appreciatively at her parents, knowing how hard they would have to struggle to make the payments, yet glad for the pleasure they derived from a small boy's happiness.

But in Mark Finley's life, the gift was to bring more than a child-tossed smile, a sweet-toned "Thank you, Grandpa." Evenings the boy listened, wide-eyed and silent, as his Catholic mother and Protestant father sat on the edge of his bed, reading the stories of Noah and Sarah and Isaac and Lot. Nightly he strained for the sound of long ago, dozing off to the rhythm of animal feet, marching two by two, seven by seven . . .

By the time Mark learned to read, he had two sisters to share his books with. Dale, born a few months before Mark's fifth birthday, was a ruddy-faced brunette, ready to take on anything that happened along the path of a determined little girl. Sandra, three years younger, looked at life through wide blue eyes—eyes that laughed and sobered, misted and sparkled, with her change of moods.

When Gloria took the children across the street to St. Patrick's Cathedral each Sunday, Jim walked six blocks to the Park Congregational church. After attending for a year, the minister asked him to teach a children's Sunday school class. Jim felt unqualified, but he accepted the challenge, and spent many an hour struggling to understand the subtle conflicts that so often surfaced in the lessons.

One Sunday, as he listened to his class repeat the Ten Commandments, a question thrust itself into his mind with such force that he could not ignore it. " *'Six days shalt thou labour, and do all thy work: but the seventh day . . .'* " The children's voices chanted on, but in Jim's mind the record was stuck at the fourth commandment. "But the seventh day . . ." That was Saturday. Then where did the first day come into the picture? Why did everyone worship on Sunday? Jim fought to resolve the apparent contradiction. Was there some other text that told of a change? Did God set apart two days each week?

57

NOBODY'S BOY

After church he walked home slowly, watching the sidewalk for the most part, trying to fit things together. For a few moments his mind went back to that evening in California nearly ten years ago. He and Gloria had been eating supper when she'd asked him about a group of men who never worked Saturdays. Jim recalled the conversation briefly, then lifted his head and hastened toward home.

Eight-year-old Mark spotted him first and broke into a run. "Guess what, Dad!"

"Well, let's see," Jim began. "Can you give me a hint?"

"I'm going to be an altar boy when I'm old enough!"

Jim stooped down even with his son and placed his hands on the boy's shoulders. "That's really good news. I'm proud of you, Mark, and I'm glad to see you're setting such a good example for your little sisters."

Basking in his father's approval, Mark began running again. shouting over his shoulder, "Beat ya home!"

"That's what you think!" Jim sprinted up beside his son just as Mark reached the front lawn. Gloria sat waiting with the girls on the porch. "Did Mark tell you the good news?" She rose and joined the two on the steps.

"Sure did, and I told him how proud I am." Jim patted Mark on the shoulder. "It's not very often a boy his age begins thinking of dedicating his life to God."

Gloria nodded, remembering the day in the rectory when the old priest had asked Jim to promise to bring his children up Catholic. He'd never gone back on his word. And his was not a grudging compromise. Long ago they had decided to send all the children to school at St. Patrick's. It seemed hard to believe that Mark was in the third grade already. Dale would be next. Gloria looked down at her brown-haired daughter, intent on a ladybug crawling across the porch. Just then the small girl jumped up and ran to her mother. "Mamma, remember that letter for Daddy?"

"Oh, yes. I forgot to give it to you yesterday, Jim. Would one of you children bring that white envelope on the bookcase?"

"I'll get it!" Mark volunteered. He was back in a few moments.

58

NEW ENGLAND TO STAY

"It's from somebody called The Bible Answers," he said, handing it to his father.

"Oh, that must be that course I sent away for a couple of weeks ago. A guy at work told me about it. Said it'd be a good way to study the Bible systematically." Jim led the way, and the others followed him into the house.

"Who's that, Jim?" Gloria asked.

"Al Lein—you know, the guy I told you about that supervises the day shift. Seems to be on the ball, that fellow. Since I went on the night shift I see quite a lot of him. We go through the schedule, and he tells me what needs to be done. Somehow we've gotten onto religion for the past couple of weeks. He doesn't push it or anything, but he sure seems to know a lot about the Bible."

After dinner Jim went back out onto the porch with his letter. The sky was overcast, the clouds as a thick gray blanket hung loosely, blocking out air and sun and warmth and light. Jim watched the clothes on the neighbor's line ripple, then jump upward with the gusts of wind. He waited for the rain to come. It began in fat, slow drops, hitting the sidewalk with determined splats, then built up to a steady parade of pounding water that soaked cement, ran down streets, and beat on the harried housewife as she unpinned her sheets and ran for the door.

Leaning back in his chair, Jim read the letter again, enjoying the feeling of being out in the storm, yet protected by the simple boards above his head.

"Is There Anything We Can Trust?" The title of the lesson stood out in bold red print. Jim read on.

The words were simple, contrasting the solid strength of the Bible with the confusion of everyday living. But to Jim the simplicity was a comfort, the message reassuring.

He read thoughtfully and carefully, and by the time he was finished, the storm had stopped. Ribbons of light curled through the parting clouds; droplets of rain glistened clear on blades of grass. Whistling, Jim folded the lesson, put it in his pocket, and walked into the house.

59

New Life at 33

"Mornin'." The man at the door smiled cordially and offered his hand. "Glad to have you with us this Sabbath."

Jim returned both the firm clasp and the smile. "My church is on summer vacation for the next two months. Friend of mine at work suggested I pay you people a visit. He lives in New London—attends the Adventist church over there."

Nodding, the older man showed Jim into the sanctuary, lowering his voice to a whisper. "Sabbath school's just barely started. Go ahead and sit anywhere."

Jim chose a pew toward the back, from which he surveyed the surroundings with surprise. The small rented room in the Masonic temple contained no more than twenty pews. A handful of people dotted the rows, their eyes directed toward a middle-aged woman behind the lectern.

". . . and we're also especially thankful for our visitors today," she was saying. "In fact, we'd like them to stand up and introduce themselves."

Glancing around, Jim noticed heads turning in his direction. People smiled encouragingly and two small girls at the front of the room stood up shyly. "We're Kathy and Cindy," the taller one managed. "We came with Mrs. Whitehead."

Now all eyes turned toward Jim. "Jim Finley," he said with a self-conscious grin. "I live over on Perkins Avenue." A touch of Brooklynese flavored the words.

"Well, we're very glad to have you Kathy, Cindy, and Jim. And we'd like to wish all our regular members a warm welcome too." The woman went on, recounting the blessings she'd received during the past week.

Jim looked around, catching the feeling of the words more

NEW LIFE AT 33

than their actual meaning. Despite the awkwardness of the previous moment, he appreciated the fact that the people here seemed to care enough to want to know his name. They seemed friendly, and eager to make him feel at home. The woman up front possessed a quality that reminded him of the impression he'd gotten after studying The Bible Answers lessons. She had that same simple strength, a warm confidence that glowed through her words.

He learned her name—Ena Hallas—and discovered that she was not the only one in that small congregation to possess such a characteristic.

Before leaving, Jim once again shook hands with the man at the door. "We'll be looking for you next Sabbath," Charlie Walker said with a confident smile.

That week Jim received another envelope from The Bible Answers. Sitting down at the kitchen table, he took out the lesson and began to read "The Man Who Was God." The words touched him, renewed him, freed something in his soul. Like the bike that had become his wings that Christmas in Brooklyn so many years ago, the message lifted him from the ordinary surroundings of everyday life, carrying him to places yet untraveled. He exulted as a boy again, with the wind on his face, pedaling yet harder, struggling to know more.

He read everything he could find after that—pamphlets, leaflets, lessons, books. And he went to church on Saturdays with rapid steps. He arrived at the Masonic temple early and listened to things he'd never heard before, struggling to fill the void that had gaped open for so long.

It couldn't be true. He studied to prove to his searching mind that the quest was useless, impossible—to end this anxious uncertainty once and for all and resume a normal life of days that passed in comfortable routine.

For two years he searched, read, prayed, sat in the front row of the little room in the Masonic temple, attended evangelistic meetings on hot summer nights. For two years he vacillated between hope and despair, questions and confidence, knowing and wondering. "Christ died for you," the evangelist intoned into the steel-sharp microphone. "He's coming again," the

61

NOBODY'S BOY

Bible assured. "He loves you," the church members beckoned.

And after two years he knew it was true. Dropping to his knees one sun-shafted morning, he prayed the words of a simple hymn:

"'I will follow Thee, my Saviour,
Thou didst shed Thy blood for me;
And though all men should forsake Thee,
By Thy grace I'll follow Thee."

The tune filled him throughout the day, playing back the words as he picked up the morning paper, mowed the lawn, headed for Bostitch and the night shift. And much later, driving home from work under a lightning-filled sky, he moved to the cadence of the chorus still. "'And though all men should forsake Thee, By Thy grace I'll follow Thee.'"

Gradually he began to catch a clue of where the words must lead. They called for action—not passive listening, not quiet humming, but standing and singing and marching to the beat. He thought of the many things he'd learned since that first morning in the Masonic temple. The fourth commandment stood out sharply. Those unchangeable words his Sunday school class had mechanically repeated that morning more than two years ago no longer sent questions waving through his mind.

"'Remember the sabbath day, to keep it holy.'" Jim spoke the words slowly, savoring their clear assurance against the mauve mist of morning. "'Six days shalt thou labour, and do all thy work: but the seventh day is the sabbath of the Lord thy God: in it thou shalt not do any work, thou, nor thy son, nor thy daughter, thy manservant, nor thy maidservant, nor thy cattle, nor thy stranger that is within thy gates: for in six days the Lord made heaven and earth, the sea, and all that in them is, and rested the seventh day: wherefore the Lord blessed the sabbath day, and hallowed it.'"

The commandment called for more than church attendance; sixty minutes of enduring the hardness of a church pew to salve the soul at the end of the week was not enough. It asked for more—much more. Put down work and bills and household jobs and *remember*. Remember that God created the world in

NEW LIFE AT 33

six literal days. Remember that God's love knows no bounds, that He voluntarily allowed His Son to be killed, loving all along the very ones who shouted "Crucify Him!" Remember that no matter how dark the day, how black the night, God still leads, still guides. Remember, like the Bible says, from "even unto even," sunset to sunset, Friday night to Saturday night.

Jim pulled the car up to the curb in front of his house. As he took the keys out of the ignition, he realized that he had just worked on Friday night for the last time in his life. It was a bit disconcerting. His young faith grabbed hold of the solid truth, but still the reality of following through pressed frightening specifics into his mind.

He couldn't expect to stop working Friday nights and stay on at Bostitch. And jobs weren't easy to come by. He'd end up out of work. And there was his wife and the three children to think of
. . .

Opening the door to the house, Jim forced himself to replace the frightening thoughts with three comforting words—God will provide.

Gloria took the news with puzzled acceptance. Her eyes registered fear, yet she struggled to keep in check the surfacing feelings. She couldn't understand it, she admitted. She needed a little time to think. But though she clung to each rosary bead a bit more tightly that evening and though her carefully powdered face could not hide her reddened lids the next morning, Gloria offered no words of discouragement.

She did not agree with everything he believed, but she loved him. And his sincerity told her that he intended to follow his convictions, regardless of anything she or others might say. Cooking breakfast Sunday morning, she determined not to do anything that would make her husband's decision any harder.

As the week wore on, Jim spent more and more time looking for a new job. On Wednesday morning, as he and Gloria sat at the kitchen table talking, the doorbell rang.

"Have you seen this ad in today's paper?" Their neighbor barely waited for the door to open before speaking. "They're looking for a setup man on automatic screw machines in Montville. Isn't that the type of work you're looking for?"

63

NOBODY'S BOY

Jim took the paper, quickly scanning the details. Within an hour he was sitting in a small office, waiting to see the manager of All-New Manufacturing. A tall dark-haired man entered the room. "I'm Bob Braman," he said, offering his hand. "I understand you're interested in work."

"Yes, sir," Jim began. "But before we even talk business, there's something I'd like to explain. The reason that I'm looking for another job is because I cannot work on Friday nights or Saturdays. If this sounds unreasonable to you, then maybe you'd like to look around for another man. If you can't find anybody else and you're willing to let me have my Sabbaths off, then give me a call." Jim rose to leave.

"Don't go." Braman motioned for him to sit down. "You may be just the man we're looking for. I'm sure we can work something out for your hours."

Jim gave his notice at Bostitch that afternoon. Driving home, he prayed for a way to break the news to Gloria. He'd be starting Monday at $100 a week. Bostitch had paid him $160. The pay cut wouldn't be easy to explain or to live with.

Gloria listened without saying a word. When he finished, her voice came out slowly, as though she fought with each syllable, not wanting to speak, yet unable to keep silent.

"We must think of the children, Jim. How can we possibly give them all they need on $240 a month less than you're making now? You know how we stretch and pull and scrimp and tear until there's nothing left to give. How can you possibly think we'll make it?" She lowered her voice slightly, looking down at the linoleum. "I'm trying to understand you, Jim. Honestly, I'm trying. But it isn't easy."

Saying nothing, Jim reached out his arms, drawing her into a tight embrace. Finally he spoke. "I've got to know that you're with me, that's all. I'm not asking you to understand. I'm just asking that you're with me."

"With you," she managed, smiling weakly. "In adversity or prosperity, till death do us part. I haven't forgotten in thirteen years." She stooped and picked up an abandoned toy race car, then looked at him squarely. "Of course I'm with you."

The night of his baptism, the words offered comfort as he

NEW LIFE AT 33

scanned the congregation. The face he longed most to see could not be there. But she was with him. Although according to Gloria's beliefs it would be a sin for her to enter a Protestant church, she was with him at home, even now. Not understanding, but accepting. Not sharing his beliefs, but supporting just the same.

The minister beside Jim in the baptismal pool lifted his hand and began to speak. "And now, James Finley, because you have decided to let Jesus be King of your life, and because you desire to follow Him all the way, I baptize you in the name of the Father, and of the Son, and of the Holy Ghost."

The cool water surged over Jim's face for a moment and then he was on his feet again—the same, yet different; guilty of sin, yet cleansed by the blood; liable to fall, yet willing to follow. Born again at 33.

No Key to Easy Street

Blue-gray mists hovered over the lake, infusing the air with a fine-cotton stillness. From the woods a phoebe whistled its two-toned song, rhythmically scolding the slumbering world. Two figures, a man and a boy, walked along the bank silently, obviously sharing the dew-washed reverence of morning. Stopping in the midst of a grove of pine trees, they put down their poles and buckets and dropped to the ground.

"Something tells me they'll be bitin' good today." Jim reached for the bucket of worms, keeping his tone low.

Mark nodded, busy with his own hook. Each year he looked forward to the first day of the fishing season, when he and his father would come to this spot and cast their lines far out into the lake. This year, about a month before trout season opened, his father had come up to his room, asking him if they could talk. Things were a little different now, he'd said. He was looking forward to going fishing, but he'd like to go the day after the season opened. Would it be OK with Mark? Saturday was a special day to him now—a day of rest and worship.

Mark straightened up and stretched his pole behind him, then snapped it forward, sending the nylon line through the air. Beside him, Jim slowly reeled in his bait. Things weren't different, Mark thought, eyeing his father's slack line. It may have been the second day of the fishing season instead of the first, but they were together, the fish would soon be biting, and there was enough bait to last all day.

But not everyone accepted Jim's change of life style so easily. That afternoon as he and Mark returned home from fishing, their next-door neighbor, a Protestant minister, asked Jim to stop by in the evening.

The last rays of sun turned the windowpane to gold as Jim

NO KEY TO EASY STREET

crossed the lawn to the minister's home. Pastor Brax wasted no time in getting to the point.

"I understand you've made a little about-face within the past few months." The words were sharp with sarcasm. "I find that too bad. As a matter of fact, I've been talking to your pastor over at the Park Congregational church and we both find that too bad. Jim, have you done any real thinking about this new religion you've fallen into?"

"More thinking than I've ever done about anything in my life."

"Then how can you allow this to happen? Can't you see that you're just using the Bible as a crutch? Look, I don't want to knock your props out from under you, but I'll tell you this much—you're doing the wrong thing."

Jim fought to keep a steady voice. "I don't understand what you mean about the Bible being a crutch."

"Then I'll tell you what I mean. The Bible was not meant just to be taken by anybody and read literally. That's dangerous. For one thing, it's filled with dirty stories—anybody who can read can find that out. And take this whole matter of you putting such ridiculous importance on Saturday worship. That alone proves that the ordinary layman has no business reading the Bible for himself. It just gets him confused."

"Pastor Brax, there's nothing confusing about the Sabbath commandment. It's all there in black and white."

"Listen, Finley"—the minister was shouting now, his face a deepening red—"if God Himself came down to this earth and told *me* what day to worship on, I'd tell Him where to go!"

Suddenly the house seemed strangely still. Jim rose to leave, and was surprised to find himself conscious of the gentle sound of a refrigerator humming, accompanied by the drip of a persistent faucet. He stepped out into the mist-laden evening, glad for the moist air that met his face. *The man needs my prayers.* He pushed back feelings of contempt, hastening toward the yellow glow shining from the windows of home. "The man needs my prayers," he breathed aloud.

Kneeling beside his bed before retiring, Jim did bring up the name of Pastor Brax. He prayed for Gloria, too—that God

NOBODY'S BOY

would bless her, guide her, give her strength to hold up under the financial pressure she didn't understand. It had been hard enough breaking the news to her about the cut in pay. But when he had begun giving his tithe and offerings, her concern deepened. Yet he could not withhold the money. He had promised God that he would follow Him, and the text in Malachi made clear what God expected of His people. "Bring ye all the tithes into the storehouse," the words read, ". . . and prove me now . . . if I will not open you the windows of heaven, and pour you out a blessing, that there shall not be room enough to receive it."

God didn't necessarily mean a material blessing, Jim thought as he rose from his knees. Christianity was certainly no key to easy street. But following the Lord meant more than extra dollars in the bank, more than the security of silver. Jim reached over and turned out the light. "Thanks for peace, God," he said, forming the words silently. "And, please, Father, bless Pastor Brax."

His prayers grew longer as the months of the Christian life progressed. He asked God to give him deeper understanding as he studied the Bible, thanked Him for prayer meeting, praised His name for the miracle of spring. And day by day his Christian strength built up, brick on brick, layer on layer. Jim Finley was constructing his spiritual foundations with careful workmanship. He would have reason to be grateful for that.

The crisis came in August, 1958. Puddles of heat shimmered on the highway, dissolving into the flat expanse of tar as Jim drove to work. He automatically turned into the gravel driveway of All-New Manufacturing, grabbed his lunch, and entered the building.

Bob Braman stood waiting for him. "I've got to talk to you about something." He led the way to the small room that served as an office. "Sit down."

"What's on your mind?" Jim pulled up a chair and faced his boss.

"You've probably noticed that things haven't been going too well in the business lately," Braman began. "Work's been

68

NO KEY TO EASY STREET

slow since last spring and it just doesn't show much sign of picking up."

Jim guessed what was coming, and looked around the room uncomfortably, studying the pattern of cracks on the plaster walls.

"There's no more work for us to give you." The words came quickly, surprisingly fast after the careful introduction. "My brother and I have talked it over. You've mentioned several times before about wanting to start a little business of your own someday. We can rent you a couple machines in the basement—give you odd jobs. It won't be easy starting out, but you'll be your own boss—can set your own hours and won't have to worry about not getting your Saturdays off, like you would if you got a job somewhere else. Take some time to think about it." He rose and opened the window, hoping to catch a stray breeze from the sultry day. "Let me know in a week or two."

Jim sat silently for a minute, then stood quickly, extending his hand. "Thanks for the offer. I'll have to do some thinking on this one."

As he operated a drill press that afternoon, Jim weighed the options. If he did take Braman up on the offer it would be rough getting started. It would be months, maybe even years, before he could make any kind of profit. And Gloria was expecting their fourth child soon. It wasn't as if he had only himself to think about.

Jim reached down for another bucket of parts, performing the job automatically, his mind racing through choices. If he didn't take Braman's offer he'd be out of a job. Then what would he do? And what about Sabbaths? How could he be sure to find work that wouldn't interfere with his keeping of the fourth commandment?

By quitting time the matter still flitted uncertainly through his mind. Yet one fact filled him with assurance. God had led him this far. And the future—though it seemed as large and uncertain as New York City had appeared to a boy from Tennessee—rested in His hands.

An empty stillness met Jim as he opened the front door to his

NOBODY'S BOY

house on Perkins Avenue. Gloria and the children had left for the island to have a campout with her parents, he remembered. He changed quickly and drove to Spicer's Pier and rented a boat. As he rowed out past the tethered boats he drank in the ocean air, thankful for its salty coolness after the burdensome heat of the August day. Overhead, gulls cried out, exultant with the smell of fish from a trawling vessel; waves lapped gently against the sides of the boat; the six-o'clock sun spread blue-gold sparkles on the surface of the water.

Jim pulled up to the rough-wood dock just in time for supper. The smell of outdoor cooking and the sight of Mark, Dale, and 4-year-old Sandra rushing down the rocky slope to greet him eased a smile onto his face.

"Can you give me a hand, Mark?" Jim threw a rope to his son, and the boy quickly secured the boat to the piling.

"When can we go fishing, Dad? I've got a whole can of night crawlers."

"How about tomorrow, son? Smells like they've got our supper ready, and then I've got to talk to your mother about something."

After the meal, Jim took Gloria aside. "As soon as we're finished cleaning up, let's ask your mother to look after the children. I'd like to go for a walk."

Later, as they sat overlooking Long Island Sound, he drew her to him. The sun slipped closer to the golden ocean, and suddenly it felt cold.

"It's about my job," he began. "Braman told me today that there's no more work." He watched her face closely, but she seemed only intent on the glowing orb of the sun—now dazzling in brilliance, now hidden by deep-velvet clouds.

"I want to start my own business, Gloria. They said they'd rent me a couple machines. It'll be rough at first, but we'll make it. I'll be able to set my own hours, run my own ship . . ." The words came as quickly as the sun dissolved into the sea. He felt almost as startled as Gloria after he'd said them. But there was no going back now.

"The Lord has led us; you know that, Gloria. Think of when I first took the job at All-New with that $60-a-week cut in pay.

70

NO KEY TO EASY STREET

Little did we know then that the company would be giving me bigger bonuses than Bostitch by the time I was through."

He stood up, studying for a moment the lights of a boat far out in the distance. Then he turned to face her again. "It's just that, well, right now it seems I have no other choice."

Gloria nodded slowly, reaching out for his hand. "The children are probably wondering what's happened to us. We'd better get back." She led the way toward camp.

One-time Altar Boy

Somehow they made it through those first years—the days of struggling and stretching and scouting for work, the weeks of praying, months of trusting. Mark Jackson, the lone employee, labored without a regular paycheck; Jim fought to keep the jobs coming, toiled to get the work done. Gloria did the clerical work at home, filing papers between calls from school about Mark and Dale, who seemed to be involved in a more-than-average number of crises, and typing letters while answering questions from Sandra and caring for Holly, who was born the same year that Finley Machine Company began operation.

And through the years of bills and child problems they emerged—a bit tired from the struggle, but whole nonetheless. A bit winded from the upstream swim, but firmer of purpose and solid of mind. The two rented machines that had marked the uncertain start of the business were replaced now by a roomful of purchased equipment. The small corner in the basement of All-New had been deserted for a first-floor shop. Gloria's father, once sole employee, received his paycheck every week with twenty-five other men.

The summer after Mark's senior year in high school, he too collected a paycheck every Thursday for work as a machine operator for the business. He had an offer to go to Florida to become the protégé of a professional golfer, and intended to put in only a few months at Finley Machine Company. Riding to work with his father on early summer mornings, he dreamed of perfect long-range shots, precision putting, the prestige of professional sportsmanship.

Jim's mind ran along other tracks. He recalled the day twenty years past, when he stood in the rectory before the old

ONE-TIME ALTAR BOY

priest and gave an easy answer to the man's question—that question that had repeated itself in brass-toned echoes for two decades. "Do you promise to bring your children up in the Catholic faith?"

Finally he gave voice to his thoughts one June morning as they drove to work. "Mark, there's something I'd like to talk to you about."

Mark turned from the blurring houses outside the window, eyed his father momentarily, then looked back to the road ahead.

"When your mother and I got married," Jim said, "I made a promise that I've never gone back on."

"What's that?" Mark sounded mildly interested.

"To rear you children as Catholics. Since your mother was marrying someone who was not of her faith, we were not allowed to have a church wedding. That's why we got married in the rectory. But before the priest would pronounce us husband and wife, I had to vow to bring all the children up Catholic. It was an easy promise to make then. I had no idea of what I really believed, and I admired your mother's strong convictions—her Christian way of doing things, her solid acceptance of God. Still do admire those things in her."

Jim paused for a minute, and turned on the windshield wiper to clear the sudden fine-tapping rain that blocked his vision.

"I never went back on my word to that priest," he went on. "I figured a promise is a promise. And, besides, I didn't want to upset your mother or confuse you children—get you caught between us.

"You're 17 now, Mark," he paused, trying to judge the meaning of his son's serious expression. "I've brought you up in the Catholic faith. And now I want to leave things up to you. If you'd like to know about my beliefs—what I understand to be true—I'd be glad to share them with you."

Jim turned the car into the driveway of Finley Machine Company. He turned off the motor, and father and son sat silently for a moment.

"I don't know, Dad." Mark's words came slowly. "I've wondered for a long time. I've wanted to know—wanted to ask

73

NOBODY'S BOY

you. But I've been afraid—afraid that maybe it would be a sin to go to church with you." His eyes shifted downward, then raised to meet his father's.

"Think about it, son," Jim reached out and touched the boy's shoulder. "You've got time."

For a week Mark mulled the issue over in his mind. He had been taught since he was 5 that it was wrong to attend another church. But just to discuss religion with his father—that was different. It would not be like going to church with him. Surely it would be all right just to ask him about what he believed, why he happened to see things the way he did . . .

"One thing I never could understand," he confessed to Jim one misty morning on the way to work. "Why is it that you go to church on Saturdays?"

The searching had begun. Morning by morning Mark asked, and mile by mile Jim explained, quoted verses, told of his own days and nights of questioning.

One day shortly before Mark's name was to be voted on as president of the Catholic Youth Organization, he left the house in early evening, heading for the rectory up the street. The sun had just set, and he walked as if in a dream, surrounded by the half-gray tones that lingered between day and night. No movement distracted his thoughts; even the air seemed unusually still.

As he knocked on the door of the rectory, Mark rehearsed the question silently one more time. If he could just get this one thing worked out. There had to be a logical explanation.

"Well, Mark!" The priest recognized him instantly. "What brings you here this evening? Something to do with your upcoming election to the CYO, no doubt. Come in, come in."

"Thank you, Father." Mark felt his small self-confidence draining away.

"Now, sit down. What can I do for you?"

"I have a question about one of our doctrines, Father." Mark pulled the words from memory, verbalizing the patterned sentences he'd gone over so many times before.

"Well, I'll be glad to straighten things out for you. What is it that seems to be confusing you?"

ONE-TIME ALTAR BOY

"It's the Sabbath commandment, Father." Mark began to repeat it slowly, but the priest stopped him.

"Yes, yes, I know the text. What is your question?"

"If the Bible says to worship on the seventh day, why do we as Catholics go to church on Sunday, the first day of the week?"

The priest stared at him incredulously for a moment. "My son, you do not treat the Bible as a set of isolated verses here and there. You treat it as a whole. There are texts in the New Testament that make the Sabbath problem perfectly clear."

"I have studied the New Testament concerning this matter, Father." Mark's voice trembled a little and he took a deep breath. "It was Jesus' custom to go into the synagogue on the Sabbath day. Paul kept the Sabbath. John refers to the Lord's day . . ." He trailed off, fearful that he had overstepped his bounds. "Could you get a Bible and help me understand these texts?"

The priest rose quickly without saying a word. He returned empty-handed, several minutes later. "I cannot seem to find a Bible. But if you can come back sometime, I'm sure we can get things straightened out."

Mark stood to leave. "Thank you, Father. I am sorry to have taken up your time."

He pushed open the heavy door and stepped into the darkness. He felt something rising and swelling in his throat. His head ached; his feet moved woodenly. No Bible in the rectory? Was the priest avoiding something, or could he really not find a Bible? Which was worse?

Gloria stood by the window watching with tear-filled eyes as her husband and son got into the car. She couldn't say anything. Mark was 17 now, and he had the right to choose to go to the Adventist church with his father, to take the Bible studies the pastor had offered to give him. *She* knew it was wrong, but it was his choice. She could only pray that he would someday confess it all.

"Mom?" Dale's tone assumed all the seriousness of a concerned 12-year-old. "My catechism teacher told me Mark will burn in hell forever and ever if he keeps on going to Daddy's

75

NOBODY'S BOY

church." Her voice broke suddenly. "Can't we stop him somehow, Mom?"

"I don't know how we can do that right now." Gloria's voice was almost a whisper. "But at least we can pray for him."

"I've written his name down in my missal." Dale's natural optimism returned. "God will answer our prayers. He always does."

But Gloria's sorrow ran deeper than the girl could realize. She cried not only for her son who might burn in hell forever, but for her mother, now lying in a hospital bed, her days numbered. The news that Eva Jackson was dying of cancer had come as a shock only weeks before. Her mother—the closest friend Gloria had ever known—was suffering, wasting away to her death.

Jim sensed the tremendous weight on Gloria's mind and watched as she fought to keep it from the children, struggling for the ready smile, the encouraging word. He wanted to take her in his arms and assure her that everything was going to be all right—that Mark was doing the right thing, and that her mother's death would be but a temporary rest, not a passage to a burning purgatory until enough prayers had been said. But the time to tell her these things was not yet. It would only add pressure to her already-burdened mind.

"Gloria," he suggested one Sunday morning in late summer, "let's take a ride over to the island. An outing will do us both good. I've been working too hard lately, and you've had a lot on your mind. We could use some salt air and sunshine."

The calls of shore birds peppered the air with staccato notes. Gloria and Jim sat high on a large rock, overlooking the dazzling Atlantic. Below, Mark helped the girls scoop and mound a castle of sand.

"I guess someday they'll discover that in more ways than one it takes only one big wave to wash years of work back into the sea." Gloria's words held no bitterness, only resignation.

"You're concerned about Mark, aren't you, Gloria?"

She nodded, and said quickly, "But I don't hold it against you. It's not your fault. You've never pushed him into anything."

"Gloria, you believe that the Lord loves you, don't you?"

76

ONE-TIME ALTAR BOY

"Yes." She gazed at the tanned children below—Sandy and Dale racing to fill their pails, Mark stooping to fix one of Holly's strawberry-blonde pigtails.

"And I believe that the Lord loves me." Jim went on. "And that He's not going to forsake us—not either one of us."

Gloria turned to face him. The words brought a gentle healing effect, like the ocean breezes cooling her tired face.

"I want to make a suggestion, Gloria. Something that we can both do for ourselves. Let's each of us pray that the Lord will lead us. We both know that He loves us. We both want to do what's right. And if we pray that kind of prayer, everything's bound to work out right."

He paused for a minute, then went on. "I don't mean right now or anything. I just mean to make it a matter of personal prayer. God wants what's right for us, so if we ask Him to lead us, He's bound to steer us onto the right track."

Gloria nodded her head, then stood up on the rock, looking far out into the ocean. The idea sounded good to her. Jim was willing to pray the same prayer; he wasn't trying to pull her into his religion—he just honestly wanted the best for both of them.

"Let's give it a try!" Her tone was brighter now, her lips curving into the hint of a smile. "Who knows? We both may end up Catholic yet!"

Mark's baptism came at the end of the summer. There were no others from the series of evangelistic meetings held that season—only Mark. But as he was lowered into the cool water, no one could know how many hundreds he himself would baptize someday.

That fall the family packed up the car to take him to Atlantic Union College—a Seventh-day Adventist school in Massachusetts. On the way back Gloria, her heart full, motioned for Jim to stop alongside a reservoir. Stepping out into the early-evening air, she turned away from the three children in the car and let the tears fall silently. *My son,* her heart spoke silently, while she was strangely aware of the sweet smell of earth and freshly cut grass, *What have I done?*

Looking at the moving water below, she knew that things

77

NOBODY'S BOY

would never be the same. When she next saw Mark, he would be changed. Life had a way of moving on, like the water, rushing always forward, and no amount of crying could ever reverse the process.

"Gloria." Jim was beside her now, looking too at the movement of the waters below. "Remember that conversation we had on the island?"

She nodded.

"Things are going to work out for us. And though it may seem unbelievable to you now, someday you're going to be proud of Mark. Real proud. We asked the Lord to take charge of our lives—to lead us. Remember? We've got to believe that He's doing that."

She nodded again, and tried to smile, but her heart was unbelievably heavy as she thought of her son left behind—the one-time altar boy who would never be the same again.

A Family United

The antiseptic smell hung heavy over the echoing corridors. Gloria counted the steps mechanically as she walked, slowing her pace as she neared the room. As she reached the door, her sister Lucy stepped into the hall.

"She seems a little better today." Lucy's optimism came through hushed tones. "She's even quite talkative."

Gloria forced a smile and stepped into the darkened room. Eva Jackson lay on her back, eyes closed, precariously plugged into life by a series of plastic tubes. Her lids flickered as her daughter approached the bed.

Gloria pulled up a chair, then reached out and took her mother's hand. "Good morning, Mother. Lucy tells me you're doing quite well today."

The thin blue lips formed a weak smile. "Yes, yes. We had a nice visit . . ."

Gloria reached up and touched her face self-consciously. "I've got new prescription sunglasses, Mother. You know how I've wanted them for years. I've got to wear them for a while so that my eyes can adjust to the lenses."

"That's real nice." The faint words trailed off, the gray eyelids flickered shut again.

The minutes ticked by rhythmically while Gloria sat beside the bed. She removed her sunglasses briefly, patting her red eyes quickly. *Adjusting to the lenses,* she thought. *Adjusting to the* illness—*the horrible, cruel, terrifying illness.* She put the glasses back on and sat silently, peering past swollen lids into the dimness.

Trays had been wheeled in and carted out by the time Gloria finally rose to leave. The corridor closed in on her like a darkened tunnel; the elevator seemed but a dimly lit box. Yet

NOBODY'S BOY

she would not share her tears with the world. Pushing the protective shell tighter to her face, she found a pay phone and fumbled in her purse for change. Then she sat down and waited for the taxi.

In the private sanctuary of her home Gloria finally removed the dark glasses and stared briefly at her swollen lids in the honest reflecting surface of the bathroom mirror. "She doesn't deserve to die," she told Jim later. "She doesn't deserve it."

Jim could bear it no longer. Holding his trembling wife, he knew what was going through her mind—the agonizing prayers for Eva Jackson, the fearful specter of death, the flames of purgatory.

"You know, death is really nothing more than a temporary sleep," he said, touching her cheek. "A rest, just a little rest, till Jesus comes."

She tightened her grip on his left hand. "How do you know that? How can you say it? It sounds so easy, so peaceful."

"I can read it to you if you'd like." More than anything he wanted to take away all the hurt, to mend her broken heart.

She nodded numbly, and he reached for his Bible and began to read from John 5. " 'Marvel not at this: for the hour is coming, in the which all that are in the graves shall hear his voice, and shall come forth; they that have done good, unto the resurrection of life; and they that have done evil, unto the resurrection of damnation.' "

"And here's the best part," he flipped the pages rapidly to the back of the Bible. "Pain is going to be over forever in the new earth. 'And God shall wipe away all tears from their eyes; and there shall be no more death, neither sorrow, nor crying, neither shall there be any more pain: for the former things are passed away.' "

Strangely comforted, Gloria crept into bed and fell into a dreamless sleep.

Eva Jackson's death came three months later, in the early spring. Later in the year Gloria and Jim moved away from the crowded neighborhood on the fringes of the city to a home quietly waiting on an acre of land. As Jim exulted in the

A FAMILY UNITED

green-gold freshness of his first country days, he had no idea that the move was to be the beginning of something far more significant than a mere change from steam-gray sidewalks to fields of dewed grass.

He was preparing for bed one evening when the unexpected, the unbelievable, came.

"I'm going to church with you tomorrow." The words were simple, as if they conveyed nothing unusual, no message of major importance. Gloria sat on the edge of the bed, hairbrush in hand, seemingly expecting no answer. She resumed brushing her short dark hair, then picked up her curler bag, leaving Jim with his own thoughts.

"Thank You, Lord." The barely audible words ascended on wings borne of ten years of faith. "Your name be praised."

He turned off the light and lay in the purple blackness of the night, not wanting to move, not daring to speak lest the tones shatter and break the sweet atmosphere that surrounded him at this moment.

He'd asked her to come to church with him only once in their twenty years of marriage. Thinking back, he recalled that the evening had been a warm one, the air limp and unmoving, like a blanket laden with unwringable moisture. "Come with me to church tomorrow," he had suggested, seeing in his mind's eye the two of them walking serenely to the Park Congregational church, the children neat and scrubbed beside them. But at the suggestion, Gloria had turned on him suddenly, without warning—a summer storm bursting unexpectedly on a sultry evening.

"The Catholic Church is my church—the only church for me. Going to another church would be turning against the very things I've cherished since I was a little girl." The words came rapidly at first, then slowed and quieted to a gentle pleading. "It would be almost like giving up my mother and father in trade for a strange set of parents. I couldn't do it. I just couldn't do it."

Jim hurt, even now, with the memory. He remembered taking her hand, squeezing it tightly, and promising himself that he would never ask her again. Ten years of Adventism had not broken the resolution. The decision, if it came, would have to be

NOBODY'S BOY

hers. Now it had happened.

Ribbons of sunlight curled through the windows the next morning, awakening Jim and Gloria to a tawny brightness. They had decided not to take the children, sensitive to their child-strong commitment to Catholicism.

In the car Gloria told Jim of the myriad fibers that had entwined silently over the years, weaving together into a sturdy cord of lengthening faith. The unconditional love he had shown her, the absence of force, his respect for her religion—all contributed to the decision she had made last evening.

"You didn't know I've been reading some of your magazines and books for quite some time now, did you?" She enjoyed the brightening of his eyes, his honest surprise that the plant of hope he'd been tending for the past decade had suddenly sprouted a shoot of living green. "But the real turn in my thinking came shortly before Mother died—when she was so terribly ill." Gloria looked downward for a moment. "I was hurting, hurting till I thought my insides would burst from the ache of wanting to make my mother well, to take away her pain . . ."

Her voice trailed off, and she mused silently for a moment before continuing. "You helped me a lot when you talked to me about death that evening, Jim. Your words soothed me, calmed my crying nerves. And afterward, when the pain had waned into numbness, the words were still there, appealing to my mind. If my church was wrong in this one thing, it wasn't infallible. I fought with this thought, wanted to reject it, but knew I had to face it. From that point on, it's been a matter of reading everything I could get my hands on that you've left around the house."

And so Jim and Gloria began attending Sabbath school and church together. On the drive to and from church, the topic of Gloria's growing interest in the Bible provided ample conversation.

Sundays, Jim drove the children to catechism, still fulfilling his promise to the old priest. He sat thinking of that priest one fall evening, trying to pull the memory of the man's face back into the realm of his consciousness. The words still beat loud in his brain, asking for his promise again and again, yet he could not

A FAMILY UNITED

see the lips that formed them, the eyes that demanded compliance. He looked up to find Dale beside him, waiting to be noticed.

"I'd like to talk to you, Dad. Can we take a walk out back or something?"

The leaves rustled beneath their feet as they climbed the hill behind the house. A bold white moon dared the stars to rival its brilliance; a blue-velvet sky provided the unbiased background.

"I've been doing a lot of thinking lately." Dale stopped at the top of the hill, lightly catching her breath. "I guess I sort of feel responsible—not only for myself but for Holly and Sandy, too."

Jim faced his 13-year-old daughter, sensing the dilemma she fought to make known, yet waiting for her to explain.

"When Mark started going to church with you, I thought he'd burn in hell if he didn't come to his senses. And now Mom . . . I'm afraid, Dad. Afraid that if I follow, Holly and Sandy will come with me and we'll all burn forever. Afraid that if I don't find out what it's all about, I'll be missing something wonderful, something that you've had ever since you started going to that church."

She stooped and picked up a leaf, and was momentarily intent on its night-muted colors. "I've got to know." She let the leaf fall slowly. "I've just got to know."

"Would you like to take studies with Mom? I don't want to pressure you, Dale, but if you could just read it for yourself, see what the Bible has to say, would that put your mind at ease?"

She thought about it for a moment, her silhouette small and dark against the expanse of hill she had just climbed. "I've always been taught that the Bible is the Word of God," she said finally. "I don't see how there could be any harm in studying it."

They ran then, red cheeked and frost crisp, to the bottom of the hill, bringing a bit of outdoors with them into the warmly lit house.

The studies began the following weekend. Mother and daughter made good students, noting the texts, questioning when confused, checking and rechecking the Biblical passages.

Autumn gusted outside the windows as they sat by the fire each evening, comparing lessons. Not content to relinquish its

NOBODY'S BOY

hold quietly, the season shrieked and crackled, garish in its final showing. December finally silenced its roaring, coating ragged leaves and blackened branches with whiteness.

Christmas was on a pure and dazzling Sabbath, with snow like lamb's wool, clumped and fleecy over the lawns. Jim sat in church, an aura of reverence and gratitude enveloping him. Outside the snow brushed colored panes of glass. At the front of the sanctuary a candle glowed, pine branches sent out a Christmas fragrance, and the organ caught the strains of "Away in a Manger."

Jim turned to look at his family beside him. Mark, home from college for the holiday break, sat with his Bible open to the Christmas story, intent on the morning passage. Holly and Sandy held their blonde heads high, Catholic-style, daring not even a whisper.

Jim turned his attention to the front of the church then, watching the velvet curtains slowly open, revealing the baptistry. Dale and Gloria faced the congregation, their baptismal robes as white as the snow drifting past the windows. A silver-gold hush fell over the church, as the pastor quietly pronounced the words of commitment, and lowered first mother, then daughter, into the water.

A simple service, a simple dedication—the culmination of years of a quiet and unpretentious love.

At the close of the service Jim made his way to the foyer where the church members were welcoming Gloria and Dale into their fellowship. He stood back, watching others shake the hands of mother and daughter, listening as they spoke the words of warmth and acceptance. Only when the last member had offered the final word of welcome did he step forward and embrace his wife and daughter.

"Merry Christmas," he said, producing corsages of red and green. And then, with an added radiance and hint of a tear, he concluded, "And happy new-birthday."

Build Your Own Dynasty

The morning sun spread a yellow glaze over the boatyard. Fishermen ambled into a doorway under a sign marked "Bait," emerging with small boxes containing their day's entertainment. Gasoline fumes blended with the tang of ocean air as motorboats pulled away from the dock, leaving a wake of white foam.

Gloria and Jim scraped at the barnacles on the bottom of the *Fin Fam,* enjoying the sights and sounds of the early season as they prepared their sixteen-foot boat for the water. Sandy and Holly jumped from rock to rock along the shore. They were the only children left at home since Dale had begun attending a Seventh-day Adventist academy in Massachusetts.

"Being by the water like this often reminds me of when I was a boy." Jim held his putty knife still for a second, then resumed scraping. "For a while my stepfather was first mate on a steamship line that traveled from New York to Savannah, Georgia. Guess I've got the ocean in my blood.

"Sometimes I wonder about my beginnings, though. You know what I mean? I've heard so many conflicting stories all my life. My mother used to tell me that my real father was some sort of civil engineer. She said he used to travel to South America and all parts of the world."

"You think there was anything to it?" Gloria shook a can of red paint vigorously, then pried off the cover.

"I doubt it. She used to come up with so many different stories I could barely keep them all straight. When she was tired of having me around, she used to sit me down and tell me that I was just a burden to David Finley, that he wasn't my real dad. Then she'd tell me that she was going to get the address of my father, so I could write to him. Said his name was Knight.

85

NOBODY'S BOY

"A couple weeks later she'd come up with another yarn. Tell me my father'd been killed somehow. I remember one time she said he was riding a horse on a plantation in South America doing some work and the horse bucked and killed him. Couple months went by and she told me it wasn't true; he was still living." Jim dipped a brush into the paint. "I've never really known what to believe."

"Is there anybody around who might know?"

Gloria's question startled him. A sea gull cried overhead, eager to catch up with the fishermen that had left it behind. Sandy and Holly laughed in the distance, dangling their toes in the biting water.

"I don't know. I've never really thought about going back and trying to find out." Jim paused. "Come to think of it, there is one person still living who might know something. I used to call her Aunt Grace. She's my stepfather's niece. She's in her late 70s, lives up in Vermont somewhere."

They pulled into the tree-lined driveway a week later, on a cloud-covered Sunday afternoon. Jim rang the bell, then stood watching the massive oak door, wondering whether it held the key to questions that had plagued him since childhood. It swung open suddenly, revealing a squat, grayish woman standing before them in a tiled foyer, adjusting a diamond earring.

"Come in," "Aunt Grace" motioned brusquely with a sweep of her fleshy arm. "I assume this is your wife, James?" Barely waiting for a nod, she ushered the way into a large old-fashioned parlor furnished in dark oak. She instructed them to be seated on a velvet wine-colored couch. Then she seated herself opposite them, in a large chair beside the fireplace.

"Well, I was quite surprised by your call," she said as she fingered the ruby pinned to her lapel. "But, then, I guess I should have expected it. You probably are aware of the fact that I have inherited some money from my husband, not to mention my sister and father."

She stood up then and stared absently through a window behind her chair, her back to Jim and Gloria. "But I have worked hard with that money, investing it, contacting brokers every day,

BUILD YOUR OWN DYNASTY

keeping up with stocks and bonds. Nothing in this life comes easy, James. You've got to work if you want to get anything out of life. Work and take a few gambles."

She whirled around suddenly, facing them with a look of intensity. "I've built my own dynasty, James. Built it brick by brick, stone by painstaking stone. It's up to you to build your own dynasty." She sat down, finished with her speech, peering at him for some kind of response.

His words came gently. "I've got my own dynasty, Grace. Four beautiful children that Gloria and I are rearing to love the Lord and to follow His leading in their lives. We didn't come here for money. I am doing well in my business. We've got a good life."

He paused then, wondering how to phrase the intent of his visit. He stood up, and walked over to a photograph on the wall, framed in ornate gold. "Your father?"

"That's right."

"I came here to ask you about *my* father, Grace. I've wondered about him all these years. Who he was, what he was like . . . I thought maybe you could provide some answers, add some pieces to the half-finished puzzle that's been baffling me for so long."

Grace joined him by the picture of her father, her look of intensity relaxing into one of bemused tolerance. "I remember the day I met your mother, James—remember it like it was yesterday. I even remember the exact dress and hat she had on."

Again she paused to look out the window, as if seeing beyond its leaden panes some picture of the past. "I also remember when she brought you to the house. Nobody knew where you came from, James. None of us could ever figure it out. And your supposed mother would never say."

Jim searched her face for some hint of meaning. "What exactly are you trying to tell me?"

"What I'm trying to say, my dear boy, is that Beulah was not your mother. We all knew that."

She drew the curtains then, shutting out the last rays of the setting sun. "It's been unseasonably chilly these past few

NOBODY'S BOY

evenings. Can I get you a hot drink?"

Later, she let them out through the oak door, clasping her shawl to her neck and signaling an abrupt farewell with her jeweled hand. "Never could figure out where that boy came from," she said to herself as the station wagon made its way back down the long driveway. "Don't know as anybody could."

She shook her head, stepped quickly into the house, and closed the door behind her, removing the afternoon's interruption from her life with a click of the lock.

Jim and Gloria drove in silence for a few miles, the blackness of the night cutting them off from any reality save the coldness of leather and the strapped-in confines of seat belts.

"Does it disturb you much?" Gloria finally asked, searching for the right words to tap his feelings.

The lights of a passing car brightened the front seat, and Jim's face showed solitary for a minute, then was lost in darkness.

"She took me by surprise, I'll have to admit. Instead of shedding some light on this whole thing, she just removed anything I thought I did know about my background. Guess I'll never know now. If Beulah wasn't my mother, I may as well forget trying to find out who my father was."

They lapsed into silence again, and then he continued. "But I learned a lot this afternoon. A lot more than Grace could ever tell me. I learned that the important thing is not where I came from, but where I am going; that it isn't going to do me any good to spend a lot of time feeling sorry for myself or worrying about who my parents were. God is my Father. He loves me, and that's all that matters.

"And I've got a family—a family that's big enough to extend around the world. All I have to do is step into an Adventist church in any town, any State, any country, and I've got Christian brothers and sisters who will welcome me as if I've spent all of my life with them.

" 'Build your own dynasty,' " he mused, reaching with his foot for the light switch. "If she could only know that God's already built it for us."

88

Sum of the Parts

FINLEY MACHINE COMPANY. Jim studied the sign on the brick building before going in, wondering for the hundredth time if he were making the right decision. The idea of selling had seemed foreign to him at first. He'd put so much of himself into the business. It was the culmination of his lifework—the end product of years of sacrifice, the sum total of a thousand decisions.

He thought back on his first job—hiding in the shadows of New York City's Pennsylvania Station, grabbing suitcases from hurried travelers and rushing them to their trains. He laughed, remembering his frantic attempts to grab the tip and take cover again before being discovered by the regular porters—the redcaps.

And that was only the beginning, he thought to himself as he walked into the shop. Waiting in his office for the prospective buyer, his thoughts spanned the years of his life from 13 to 55, remembering other jobs, too. Leading the blind lady who made slipcovers in and out of Broadway theaters. Scraping chewing gum off of classroom floors. Loading clay pigeons on skeet traps at the Brooklyn gun club. Delivering groceries. Killing and dressing chickens.

His thoughts came as rapidly as a spliced reel of old film, producing staccato memories on a stretched canvas screen. There were the hours spent stocking shelves in a New Jersey supermarket. The days when he set up wooden bottles on a table after they'd been knocked down with softballs by nickel-paying customers at an amusement park. The weeks with the New York City Postal Telegraph, running errands for the business world, singing telegrams, and even walking dogs.

Jim looked through the window of his office at the men

NOBODY'S BOY

operating the drill presses and thought back on the first savings account he'd had and the pride he'd taken in cashing his paycheck. Twelve dollars a week pay. It had seemed almost like twelve hundred, he mused. And the single dollar bill he had so proudly deposited at Chase Manhattan Bank each Thursday. It seemed incredible now that it had given him such a feeling of security.

The door to the office opened, and the flow of memories was cut off, as if the plug had been pulled and the reel of film suddenly had been made motionless.

"Good morning." Jim stood up and extended his hand to a man about twenty years younger than himself.

"Have a seat."

When the transaction had finally been made, after weeks of discussion and deliberation, Jim breathed a sigh of relief. The contract was a simple one—no down payment, easy terms, the price lower than appraised. But the thought of unloading the twenty-four-hour pressure of running a business gave him a spirit of optimism.

"It's about time I slowed down," he told Gloria as they sorted through some last-minute paper work. "Can you imagine me putting in just forty hours a week after all these years? It's hard to believe, but I guess at my age I have it coming."

"You deserve it!" Gloria put down a stack of papers and smiled at him. "If anybody deserves it, you do. You've certainly put in your share of time over the years!"

He nodded, thinking ahead to the life style awaiting him. Once again the reel of film began spinning, but this time with a far different picture—not spliced and flickering, like the other, but full-color, bright, and smooth. He saw himself working with a few machines in the basement of his home, taking things at a leisurely pace. He thought ahead to the Bible studies he'd be able to give, the Sundays out on the boat, the evenings free from paper work and blueprints.

The transition would come over a period of time. The contract stated that Jim would be employed by Finley Machine Company for a year, helping the new owner become

90

SUM OF THE PARTS

established. It would be a good year, he decided—a time to loosen gradually the taut reins that had calloused his hands and mind for so long. A time to thank the Lord for the blessings the business had brought to his family—the living it had provided, the needs it would continue to meet.

Jim began his new role on a blustery day in October, reporting to the office for his assigned duties. Day by day he fulfilled the tasks outlined for him. Yet working beside the men, carrying out orders, he sensed that something was wrong. Somehow things were not exactly as they should be. He said nothing, but wondered as he was told to sweep the floor rather than asked to consult on orders. One Monday morning after he had been assisting the new owner for three months, Jim arrived at work at seven o'clock to find the owner waiting for him in the office.

"My attorney is on the phone," he said as he handed Jim the receiver. "He'd like to talk to you."

"This is Jim Finley." Jim held the receiver loosely, leaning against the side of the desk.

"Yes, Mr. Finley. I'll try to make this as brief as possible so as not to take up too much of your time." The voice on the other end sounded programmed. "The new stockholders of Finley Machine Company held a meeting over the weekend. It was decided that you are no longer needed. Please leave the company as soon as you can gather up any personal materials you might have around."

Jim turned to the owner in disbelief. There was a click on the other end of the line, followed by a rasping tone.

"I don't understand," he began, but saw the futility of words in the determined stance of the man who now gave orders.

"Today, Jim," said the new owner, pointing to the door of the office. "And close that door behind you when you go out."

Dazed, Jim descended the stairs, picked up his toolbox and headed for the door. He looked behind him once, caught a glimpse of one of the men dropping a time card into the box, and then turned and walked out, leaving behind a life's work, the dream-come-true of a boy from the slums. He drove home as if in a dream, the sum of the parts splashing kaleidoscopic scenes

91

NOBODY'S BOY

before his eyes. It was not twenty years. It was forty. It was Hell's Kitchen. It was Harlem. It was the War Years—the struggle starting the business, skimping to meet the payroll, learning about Government red tape, taxes, regulations, workers' compensation, insurance.

It was listening to marital problems, spiritual problems, health problems. It was coming to after surgery and being greeted by a foreman holding blueprints.

It was giving work to college students from the church in the summer, being able to support the church with money, educating four children through college.

It was only eight o'clock when Jim pulled into the driveway. "Well, Gloria," he said, catching the surprise on her face as he swung open the kitchen door, "I guess we'll be putting our energies into that new little business sooner than we thought."

The year that followed pressed down upon them like a heavy blanket, sodden with an undeserved weight. No money came in the mail for the purchase of Finley Machine Company. No working capital provided the framework for the fledgling business they sought to establish to provide a living. Starting with a patent he had purchased two years before, Jim spent months developing a system to manufacture specialized exercise bicycles. But lack of money forced cold reality, and to avoid ever-threatening bankruptcy, he sold the business to pay the debts incurred in its development.

Operating a few machines, he and Gloria battled to weave the frayed ropes of their finances back together, while forces pulled from all sides. The contract Jim had signed when selling Finley Machine Company forbade him to enter into competition with the new owner. The specifics set down a limited number of production workers he could hire.

Getting up at five o'clock each morning, Jim and Gloria prepared for a long day's work. To keep the needed production up, both operated machines until late in the evening, but they still found time to give Bible studies to an interested family in the community.

And over all, like a cloud of unknown density, hung the question of justice that had not been dealt out. Lawyers and

SUM OF THE PARTS

accountants whirled about them in a maze of months, but after three years, the initial payments for a life's work were still no more than a haze-filtered dream.

Jim wrestled, inwardly, seeking to understand the injustice, to learn to love the man whose actions he could not comprehend. "Love your enemies," he read for worship. And he prayed. He paced. He pleaded for pardon for those involved, yet something within cried for respite of his own agony. The boy who had learned that first lesson in Brooklyn so many years ago even now came to the surface with his taunts, calling for fairness, demanding that the score be evened, urging him to hurt as he had been hurt.

But the taunts were only that—schoolboy cries, weak and unable to prevail above the steadying voice of the Master.

And as the breezes of spring swept a comforting warmth into the air, things began to take on a new perspective. Circumstances did not change, but they were viewed in the light of a larger reality. Total reimbursement for twenty years of labor did not suddenly appear. The prayed-for case did not come before the courts. Yet a sense of peace, solid and sure, infiltrated Jim's being.

Selling a few orders week after week, he learned to look beyond the temporal things, knowing that even yet the Lord would push back the debris from his path. When the bill came for the last year of Holly's college education, Gloria's sister, Lucy, lent them the money. When tax time rolled around, a check appeared in the mail for the exact amount. A forgotten debt was being repaid just when it was needed.

But the experience provided more than a reassurance of physical things. It refreshed the spirit of his life with a clean understanding of others, a kinship with suffering, a knowledge of trust.

A business had been lost. Twenty years of struggle. A lifetime of calluses. Two hands full of knicks and scratches.

And in its place an intangible had been gained. The assurance of comfort. An aura of peace. Two hands, emblazoned with scars borne of nails, stretching from heaven to steady his steps.

Happiness

ttention, passengers. Please notice that the no-smoking light has been turned on and also the signal for fastening your seat belts. We ask that you observe these regulations until you see the signal lights go off. We will be taking off within the next minute and will be arriving in Los Angeles at three o'clock Pacific time. Have a pleasant trip."

Jim leaned back in his seat. Beside him Gloria and Lucy looked over the menus handed them by the stewardess. Suddenly the motors became more intense, the ground's scenery sped by, and with a feeling of lightness, the plane lifted from the earth.

Looking down on New York City, Jim felt as if his life were being marked out in sharp blocks below him. New York City—the scene of his boyhood—a living, breathing, screaming reality that had threatened to swallow him up with its demands.

The blocks below grew smaller as he watched, shrinking first to toy-sized squares, then to oblivion. The significance of the city had lost its impact, seemed nothing more than a farce compared to the vastness of the sky he now flew.

His life, he mused, had become filled with something far more vital than anything he could have drawn from the city. And that not by mere coincidence. The circumstances surrounding his conversion had been no chance happenings. The pattern of his days had been as intricate as a spider web, the tiny filaments weaving, forming, until the Master Artist had spun them to completion.

He thought of the specifics, watching the reflection of the sun as it glistened from the wing of the plane. The job transfers at Bostitch, ultimately leading him to the man who would sit down and open the Bible before him. The training he'd picked up in

HAPPINESS

the Navy that eventually enabled him to set up his own machine shop. The opportunities that business had afforded him.

Jim stood up for a minute, reaching for the wallet in his back pocket. Settling back into his seat, he pulled out a small stack of photographs. A simple white church, its spire piercing upward toward an azure sky, lay on top of the pile. "That small room in the Masonic temple," he mused. "Who would have ever guessed the numbers that would be added to the pews, the excitement we would feel over our own building?"

He put the picture on the bottom of the pile and mused on the individual pictures of his children and their families.

Mark, his wife, Teenie, and their three children smiled confidently at him from a background of muted rose. Jim thought of the many chapters of their ministry thus far—the pastoral work, the teaching, the evangelistic meetings. His grip tightened on the picture for a second as he prayed for continued blessings on their work.

He looked at Dale and David, next, with their two children, and he laughed, thinking of the latest antics of the younger girl. "Keep it up, kid," he admonished the red-haired child grinning mischievously at him from the photo. "That's what got your mother through a lot of tight situations." He thought back on Dale's early years of conversion—her willingness to be different, to stand up for what she believed in. He remembered the sermons she had given as a student at Pioneer Valley Academy, the office of class pastor she had held. His thoughts continued on, flashing pictures of Dale leading out in Sabbath school, David teaching in the church school.

The plane caught an air pocket then, thudding against the wind as he pulled out the photo of Sandy and her husband, Eric. Their service is just beginning, he mused. Just two more months and they would be out of the Seminary, ready to begin their work in up-State New York.

He looked at Holly, last of all, her countenance glowing against a background of mauve. Holly Finley, registered dietitian. Never thought I'd be the father of such a prestigious young lady, he chuckled. The last one to graduate—it's hard to believe I'm finally making this trip after four children and all

95

NOBODY'S BOY

these years. In just a few days the last one will be marching down the aisle for that diploma.

Jim took a deep breath, then replaced the pictures and turned to face the silver-blue sky. Happiness—I've lived a long time to understand it. Four children: far from perfect, but struggling to do what's right. A glistening white church: not filled with saints, but overflowing with those on their way. A worn black Bible: not an instrument of legalistic facts, but brimful of assurances of the love of God.

He closed his eyes, dozing off while States rolled by in crazy-quilt pattern far below. The public address system awakened him, with its end-of-trip instructions. "We are now approaching Los Angeles International Airport. Before you leave, please be sure to check the racks for any personal items you might have stored there. Have a pleasant day."

Jim stepped out into the aisle after Gloria and Lucy. Entering the terminal building, he had a brief flicker that he had lived the moment before in some remote corner of his being. He remembered stepping off a train, gripping the railing with sweaty palms, desperately searching the crowd for a face that meant home. People, more people than he had ever seen before, milled about in every direction.

A woman passed by, her steps labored and heavy. He remembered, then, that day so long ago in New York City. The search of a young boy for a mother and father.

With confident step he rushed to meet his daughter, her arms already stretching to embrace mother and aunt. And then, like an objective bystander, he stood back, viewed the road that had taken him from Hell's Kitchen, carried him past Harlem, into this very moment, and knew—with the most blessed assurance— the meaning of his heritage.